EXPLRING

GERMAN

Second Edition Revised

Joan G. Sheeran
J. Patrick McCarthy

Consultant
Wolfgang S. Kraft

D1366457

EMC/Paradigm Publishing, Saint Paul, Minnesota

Illustrator *Jackie Urbanovic*
Cover Design *Jennifer Wreisner*

Photos Credits
Austrian National Tourist Office: x (bottom left), xi (top left)
Deutsche Bahn: 146 (top left)
Deutsche Post: 26 (top left)
Ernst Klett International GmbH: 15 (top left)
Fremdenverkehrs- und Kongressamt Leipzig: vii (bottom left)
Fremdenverkehrsverband Franken e.V.: vi (top left), xii (center right)
German Information Center: vii (top)
Kraft, Wolfgang: iii, viii (top right and bottom), ix (all), 7 (bottom left and right), 19 (all)
Kurverwaltung Bodenmais: viii (top left), xii (top left)
Kurverwaltung Garmisch-Partenkirchen: vi (bottom left)
Quelle AG, Nürnberg, Germany: 15 (top right), 41 (top left and bottom right), 78 (center left and bottom), 85 (top left, bottom left and right), 91 (top right and bottom left)
Städtisches Verkehrsamt Lichtenfels: vii (bottom right)
Stadtwerbung und Touristik Münster: xii (bottom left)
Touristikverband Schleswig-Holstein: 37 (top left)
Verkehrs- und Reisebüro Gemeinde Oberammergau: x (center right)
Verkehrsamt Cottbus: x (top left)
Verkehrsamt Oppenau: xi (center right)
Verkehrsamt Reit im Winkl: 1 (center right)
Verkehrsamt Saarburg: xi (bottom left)

The publisher would also like to thank the numerous tourist offices in Germany, Austria and Switzerland which supplied realia used at the end of each chapter.

ISBN 0-8219-2405-2

Published by EMC/Paradigm Publishing
875 Montreal Way
St. Paul, Minnesota 55102
800-328-1452
www.emcp.com
E-mail: educate@emcp.com

Printed in the United States of America
1 2 3 4 5 6 7 8 9 10 XXX 07 06 05 04 03 02

INTRODUCTION

Hallo und willkommen!

Hello and welcome! Did you know that one out of every four Americans are of German ancestry? Even if you aren't from a German background, you are probably curious about exploring a world where over 100 million people communicate in German every day. Many of these German speakers deal with Americans, since Germany is the United States' largest trading partner in Europe. In *Exploring German* you will learn some common words and expressions that these people use daily. If you learn these basic words and expressions, and if you have the opportunity to travel to one of the European countries where people speak German, you will be able to understand some of the things they say. They will also be able to understand you. As the world continues to shrink and as countries and people grow closer and closer together, it is important to be able to communicate with each other.

If you practice correct pronunciation with your teacher or with the recordings, you will learn to speak German even better. Besides being able to understand and speak basic German, you will find out some information about Germany and get some insight into the country's rich traditions in art, music and literature. Hopefully, throughout your journey you will discover that learning German is fun and not too difficult. Be sure to practice your German at every opportunity both in and outside of class. As with any other skill, the more you practice, the better you will become.

So, let's get started! *Also, los!*

Table of Contents

Exploring

...countries and cities

Nürnberg, Germany

Reit im Winkl, Germany

Garmisch-Partenkirchen, Germany

Baden-Baden, Black Forest, Germany

Lichtenfels, Germany

Leipzig, Germany

Maikammerer Straße

Das Landhotel garni
Familie Gernert

◀ ⚽/ Grillhütte

◀ Pfarrzentrum

◀ ✕ Altes Rathaus

◀ ✕ Ratsschenke

◀ 🛏 Grüner Baum

◀ ✕ Gasthaus-Café
Dalberg

◀ Hotel-Restaurant ✕
St. Martiner Castell

◀ Verkehrsamt ℹ

◀ 3 km PWV-Rasthaus
an den Fichten

◀ ✕ Pension
Bergel

◀ Park-Café

◀ ✕ Wappen-
schmiede

◀ ✕🛏 Hotel-Restaurant
Haus am Weinberg

◀ Weinstube
Krabbenescht

◀ Hotel-Restaurant
Haus am Rebenhang ✕

Fahr
vorsichtig

Es könnte auch
Dein Kind sein

BÄCKEREI

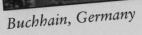

Buchhain, Germany

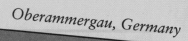

Oberammergau, Germany

Wien, Austria

Wien, Austria

Oppenau, Germany

Saarburg, Germany

...and culture.

Bodenmais, Germany

Germany

Münster, Germany

GREETINGS AND COURTESY
Begrüßungen und Höflichkeit

Guten Morgen.
Good Morning.
Guten Tag.
Hello.
Guten Abend.
Good Evening.
Gute Nacht.
Good Night.

Höflichkeit

Bitte. ——— Please.
Danke. ——— Thank you.
Bitte (schön). — You're welcome.
Entschuldigung.-Excuse me.
Es tut mir Leid.-I'm sorry.

Tag. ——— Hi.
Auf Wiedersehen.—Good-bye.
Bis später. — See you later.
Bis morgen.— See you tomorrow.

Ja.

Nein.

Viel Glück.

GOOD LUCK!

Wie heißt du?
What's your name?

Ich heiße Josef.
My name is Josef.

Du sprichst deutsch, nicht wahr?
You speak German, don't you?

Ja. Ich spreche deutsch.
Yes. I speak German.

Wie geht's?
How are you?

Gut, danke,
Und dir?
Fine thanks. And you?

Nicht schlecht.
Not bad.

Angenehm.
Es freut mich.
I'm pleased to meet you.

Sprichst du deutsch?
Do you speak German?

Nein. Ich spreche nicht deutsch.
No. I don't speak German.

 Tschüs = So long.   Spanisch (Spanish), Französisch (French), Englisch (English), Italienisch (Italian), Russisch (Russian)

Höflichkeit ist Trumpf.   Courtesy is power.

Ich heiße...

Antje	Andreas
Bettina	Dieter
Brigitte	Erich
Christl	Franz
Erika	Fritz
Evelyn	Günter
Gisela	Heinz
Heidi	Holger
Julia	Hans
Jutta	Josef
Karin	Kurt
Luise	Lars
Maria	Manfred
Marianne	Michael
Martina	Patrick
Monika	Robert
Renate	Rudolf
Rita	Stefan
Sabine	Werner
Susanne	Willi

Exercises

A Wähle das nicht zutreffende Wort! *Choose the word which does not fit.*

1. Nacht	Morgen	Tag	Glück
2. deutsch	nein	englisch	französisch
3. Angenehm.	Bis später.	Tschüs	Auf Wiedersehen.
4. Bitte.	Danke.	Bitte sehr.	Ja.
5. Wie heißt du?	Wie geht's?	Nicht wahr?	Sprichst du spanisch?

B Wähle nur Mädchennamen. *Choose only girls' names.*

1. Gisela
2. Heinz
3. Günter
4. Bettina
5. Sabine
6. Christl
7. Werner
8. Dieter
9. Luise
10. Andreas

C Beantworte die Fragen auf Deutsch! Schreib deine Antworten! *Answer the questions in German. Write your answers.*

1. Wie geht's? _____

2. Sprichst du deutsch? _____

3. Wie heißt du? _____

D   Schreib zu jeder Abbildung einen Ausdruck auf deutsch! *Write in German an expression that corresponds to each illustration.*

1. _____

2. _____

3. _____

4. _____

5. _____

6. _____

7. _____

E Short Answers (Auf Deutsch, bitte.).

1. How do you wish someone "good luck"?

   _____

2. *"Tag"* is a short version of

   _____

3. How do you greet someone in the morning?

   _____

4. How do you greet someone in the evening?

   _____

5. How do you say "good-bye"?

   _____

6. *"Nein"* is the opposite of

   _____

7. An expression at an introduction is

   _____

8. Answer this question: *"Wie geht's?"*

   _____

9. Do German speakers tend to shake hands more frequently than Americans?

   _____

10. "Please" means _____

F Beantworte die Fragen auf Deutsch! *Answer the questions in German.* Schreib deine Antworten. *Write your answers.*

1. Werner: Guten Morgen, Angelika. Wie geht's?

   Angelika: _____

2. Heidi: Sprichst du englisch, Markus?

   Markus: _____

3. Günter: Tag! Ich heiße Günter. Wie heißt du?

   Luise: _____

Kreuzworträtsel

G

Vertical

1. opposite of "ja"
2. "Du sprichst deutsch, nicht...?"
4. expected response to a favor
6. sometimes needed at exam time
7. opposite of "Nacht"
8. "Ich... (My name is)" Note: ß = ss
10. "...geht's?"
11. "Ich...deutsch."
12. "Abend" auf englisch
16. "Wie heißt...?"

Horizontal

3. normal evening greeting
5. opposite of "Tag"
6. opposite of "schlecht"
9. said when departing
13. German word for "I"
14. "...Glück."
15. courteous request
17. spoken in Austria, Switzerland and Germany
18. part of the day in which school begins

CLASSROOM OBJECTS
Die Klasse

Was ist das?
Das ist ein...
Das ist eine... } What is this? (that) This is a...

eine Karte — a map

eine Wand — a wall

ein Klassenzimmer — a classroom

ein Fenster — a window

eine Uhr — a clock

ein Bild — a picture

eine Spitze — a point

ein Bleistift — a pencil

ein Radiergummi — an eraser

eine Tafel — a board

ein Spitzer — a pencil sharpener

eine Fahne — a flag

ein Stuhl — a chair

ein Wischer — an eraser

Kreide — chalk

ein Schreibtisch — a desk

ein Bücherschrank — a bookcase

ein Buch — a book

ein Blatt Papier — a sheet of paper

ein Heft — a notebook

ein PapierKorb — a wastebasket

ein Lineal — a ruler

ein Kuli — a ballpoint pen

ein Stück Kreide = a piece of chalk, eine Klasse = class of students (also: classroom) Kuli = short form of "Kugelschreiber."

Wände haben Ohren.   Walls have ears.

Exercises

A Your teacher will point out 24 classroom objects. As your teacher pronounces each object in German, find it on the list below and place the appropriate number after it.

eine Spitze _____   ein Stück Kreide _____

ein Stuhl _____   ein Fenster _____

ein Kuli _____   eine Wand _____

ein Lineal _____   ein Schreibtisch _____

ein Blatt Papier _____   ein Heft _____

eine Karte _____   eine Uhr _____

ein Klassenzimmer _____   ein Spitzer _____

ein Wischer _____   ein Bild _____

eine Klasse   eine Fahne _____

ein Radiergummi _____   ein Bücherschrank _____

ein Buch _____   eine Tafel _____

ein Papierkorb _____   ein Bleistift _____

B Answer each question in English.

1. Where in the classroom is the "Fahne"?

   _____

2. How many "Fenster" are in this room?

   _____

3. What is the color of the "Tafel"?

   _____

4. Is the "Klassenzimmer" big or little?

   _____

5. What is kept in a "Bücherschrank"?

   _____

C Wähle die richtige Antwort! *Choose the correct response.*

1. Ink is used in a...
   a. Kuli   b. Bleistift

2. One sits on a...
   a. Stuhl   b. Schreibtisch

3. In order to write on the board one needs some...
   a. Kreide   b. Wand

4. Minutes and hours are indicated by the...
   a. Papierkorb   b. Uhr

5. A student writes assignments in a...
   a. Heft   b. Bleistift

6. In order to draw a straight line one uses a...
   a. Wischer   b. Lineal

D Schreib den deutschen Namen von jedem Objekt! *Write the German name of each object.*

1. _____

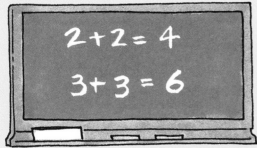

2. _____

3. _____

4. _____

5.

6. _____

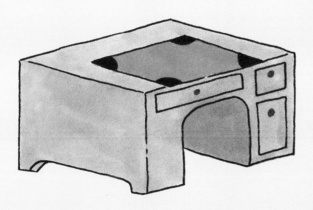

7. _____

8. _____

9. _____

10. _____

11. _____

12. _____

13. _____

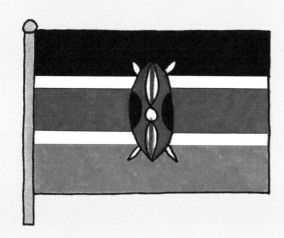

14. 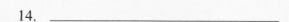_____

15. _____

E Ergänze die Sätze! *Complete the sentences.*

1. _____ ist das?

2. Das _____ ein Kuli.

3. Das ist _____ Fahne.

4. Das ist _____ Buch.

F Ergänze die fehlenden Buchstaben! *Complete the missing letters.*

1. Tafe___	9. Fe___ster	17. Radierg___mmi
2. B___ld	10. Kart___	18. Bu___h
3. Wa___d	11. L___neal	19. Wi___cher
4. ___reide	12. S___itzer	20. Pap___er
5. Schrei___tisch	13. U___r	21. Klassen___immer
6. ___leistift	14. Fa___ne	22. Bücherschran___
7. Stuh___	15. Kul___	23. K___asse
8. Papierk___rb	16. ___eft	24. Sp___tze

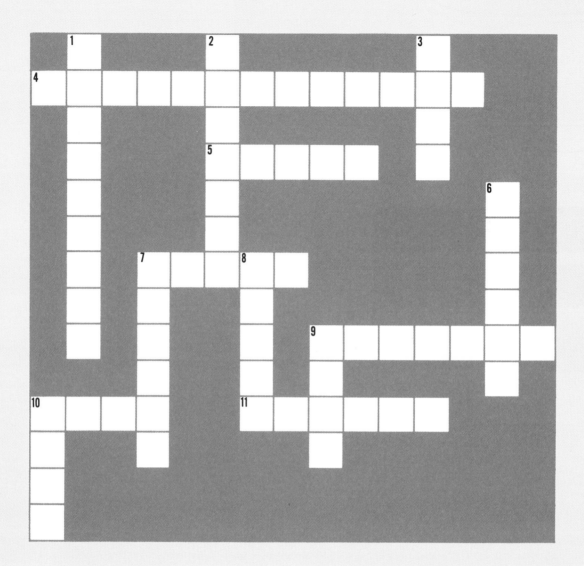

G

Vertical

1. writing instrument
2. where light is admitted
3. contains notes and assignments
6. lined or plain
7. white writing instrument
8. used with chalk
9. side of a room
10. source of information

Horizontal

4. place for instruction
5. place to sit
7. representation of geographical areas
9. used to erase the board
10. wall decoration
11. straight edge

DEUTSCH
5. KLASSE

TIM 7
...UND DER GESANDTE DER UNO

Ubi Soft   HEUREKA

MATHE
6. KLASSE

TIM 7
...UND DAS PREISAUS-
SCHREIBEN IN NEW YORK

Ubi Soft   HEUREKA

ENGLISCH
6. KLASSE

TIM 7
UND DER GRENKENRAUCH ...

Ubi Soft   HEUREKA

ENGLISCH
5. KLASSE

TIM 7
...UND DER VERIRRTE KURIER

Ubi Soft   HEUREKA

③ **89**95
Sammies by Samsonite®

Galaxy

④ **22**95
Schüler-Etui

Wild Horses

STAEDTLER® Kiddi

MEIN STUNDENPLAN

	MONTAG	DIENSTAG	MITTWOCH	DONNERSTAG	FREITAG	SAMSTAG
8⁰⁰-8⁴⁵	Mathe	Chemie	Deutsch	Erdkunde	Englisch	
8⁵⁰-9³⁵	Deutsch	Biologie	Englisch	Informatik	Französisch	
9³⁵-9⁵⁰	Große Pause					
9⁵⁰-10³⁵	Englisch	Sport	Biologie	Kunst	Mathe	
10⁴⁵-11¹⁵	Erdkunde	Sport	Geschichte	Französisch	Deutsch	
11²⁵-11⁴⁰	Große Pause					
11⁴⁰-12²⁵	Französisch	Mathe	Physik	Chemie	Physik	
12³⁰-13¹⁵		Musik		Englisch	Geschichte	

CLASSROOM COMMANDS
Imperative in der Klasse

Wiederhole !
Repeat.

Sprich!
Speak.

Sag das auf Deutsch!
Say that in German.

Ergänze die Sätze!
Complete the sentences.

Beantworte die Frage!
Answer the question.

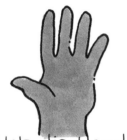

Heb die Hand!
Raise your hand.

Nimm Papier heraus!
Take out paper.

Mach das Buch auf!
Open the book.

Mach das Buch zu!
Close the book.

Schreib!
Write.

Hör zu!
Listen.

Lies!
Read.

Setz dich!
Sit down.

Ergänze die Sätze!
Complete the sentences.

Geh an die Tafel!
Go to the board.

 Was Hänschen nicht lernt, lernt Hans nimmermehr.

As the twig is bent, so grows the tree.

Exercises

A Do what your teacher commands.

B Schreib auf Deutsch, bitte! *Write in German, Please.*

1. (Speak.) _____

2. (Say.) _____

3. (Complete.) _____

C Do what the following command orders you to do.

Schreib deinen Namen! _____

D Was passt zusammen? *What matches?*

A		**B**
1. schreiben _____		a. to repeat
2. gehen _____		b. to write
3. lesen _____		c. to lift, raise
4. wiederholen _____		d. to read
5. heben _____		e. to go

E Schreib einen deutschen Befehl zu jeder Abbildung. *Write a German command for each illustration.*

1. _____

2. _____

3. _____

4. _____

5. _____

F Ergänze jeden Satz. *Complete each sentence.*

1. _____ Papier heraus.

2. Sag das _____ Deutsch.

3. _____ dich.

4. Mach das _____ zu.

5. _____ die Hand.

6. Ergänze die _____.

7. _____ das Buch.

G Wähle den zutreffenden Befehl! *Choose the corresponding command.*

1. Write.   (Sprich!   Schreib!   Hör zu!)
2. Raise.   (Heb!   Lies!   Mach zu!)
3. Speak.   (Geh!   Ergänze!   Sprich!)
4. Say.   (Mach auf!   Setz dich!   Sag!)
5. Take out.   (Nimm heraus!   Hör zu!   Geh!)

Betreten auf eigene Gefahr

Fußgänger
bitte gegenüberliegende
Straßenseite benutzen

Parken
VERBOTEN

Einfahrt freihalten

Parkschein-
automat

Hier
Parkschein
lösen

1814

Radfahrer
bitte
absteigen

4

NUMBERS

Zahlen

Wie viel ist...?   How much is...?

1 eins
2 zwei
3 drei
4 vier
5 fünf

6 sechs
7 sieben
8 acht
9 neun
10 zehn

11 elf
12 zwölf
13 dreizehn
14 vierzehn
15 fünfzehn

16 sechzehn
17 siebzehn
18 achtzehn
19 neunzehn

20 zwanzig
21 einundzwanzig
22 zweiundzwanzig
23 dreiundzwanzig
24 vierundzwanzig
25 fünfundzwanzig
26 sechsundzwanzig
27 siebenundzwanzig
28 achtundzwanzig
29 neunundzwanzig

30 dreißig
31 einunddreißig
32 zweiunddreißig

40 vierzig
41 einundvierzig
42 zweiundvierzig

50 fünfzig
51 einundfünfzig
52 zweiundfünfzig

60 sechzig
61 einundsechzig
62 zweiundsechzig

70 siebzig
71 einundsiebzig
72 zweiundsiebzig

80 achtzig
81 einundachtzig
82 zweiundachtzig

90 neunzig
91 einundneunzig
92 zweiundneunzig

100 hundert
200 zweihundert
1.000 tausend

Ein Narr kann mehr fragen als sieben Weise sagen.

One fool can ask more questions than seven wise men can answer.

Supplementary Vocabulary

Exercises

A After you study the numbers and practice saying them, try to write these numbers from memory. (Auf Deutsch, bitte.)

1 _____   6 _____

2 _____   7 _____

3 _____   8 _____

4 _____   9 _____

5 _____   10 _____

B Rate yourself. How did you do? Circle your evaluation.

1. very well   2. fairly well   3. poorly

C Practice again. Schreib die Zahlen! *Write the numbers.*

    Beispiel: zwei ___2___

1. fünf _____   4. neun _____

2. acht _____   5. sieben _____

3. eins _____

D Schreib das deutsche Wort für jede Zahl!

3 _____   6 _____

4 _____   10 _____

E Tell whether the following equations indicate addition, subtraction, multiplication or division.

1. Vierzehn geteilt durch sieben ist zwei. _____

2. Zwei und zehn ist zwölf. _____

3. Acht mal drei ist vierundzwanzig. _____

4. Neunzehn weniger dreizehn ist sechs. _____

F Try once more to write the numbers in German. (Auf Deutsch, bitte.)

8 _____ 3 _____ 10 _____ 1 _____ 9 _____

2 _____ 5 _____ 4 _____ 7 _____ 6 _____

G Wie viele Objekte gibt es hier? *How many objects are pictured? Write the number in German.*

= _____

= _____

= _____

= _____

= _____

H Wie viele Objekte gibt es zusammen? *How many* _____
objects are there altogether?

Now, write this sum in German. _____

I Schreib die Antworten auf Deutsch!
  Beispiel: 6 − 4 = <u>zwei</u>

1. 12 × 4 = _____

2. 30 − 10 = _____

3. 8 − 6 = _____

4. 12 + 18 = _____

5. 100 ÷ 2 = _____

6. 60 + 10 = _____

7. 30 − 15 = _____

8. 80 ÷ 2 = _____

9. 10 × 10 = _____

10. 15 + 4 = _____

J Your teacher will say ten numbers in German. Write the corresponding numbers.

1. _____   6. _____

2. _____   7. _____

3. _____   8. _____

4. _____   9. _____

5. _____   10. _____

K How many interior angles are there in each design? Circle the number.

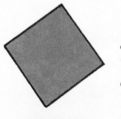

vier
acht
zehn
drei

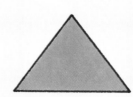

fünf
drei
vier
sieben

sieben
sechs
elf
fünf

fünf
neun
acht
elf

L Lies den Absatz! *Read the paragraph. Dann wähle die richtigen Antworten!*

Im Klassenzimmer gibt es viele Objekte. Es gibt fünfundzwanzig Stühle, vier Fenster, sieben Wischer, neunzehn Hefte und eine Karte. Ein Stuhl kostet siebenundzwanzig Dollar. Ein Wischer kostet fünfunddreißig Cent und eine Karte kostet vierzig Dollar.

1. Im Klassenzimmer gibt es...Objekte.
   - a. wenige
   - b. viele
   - c. acht
   - d. zehn

2. Es gibt insgesamt (totally)...Objekte.
   - a. einundvierzig
   - b. achtunddreißig
   - c. sechsundfünfzig
   - d. dreiundzwanzig

3. Wie viel kostet ein Stuhl?
   - a. $27.00
   - b. $35.00
   - c. $40.00
   - d. $25.00

4. Wie viele Hefte gibt es?
   - a. 53
   - b. 7
   - c. 25
   - d. 19

5. Wie viele Fenster gibt es?
   - a. 19
   - b. 25
   - c. 4
   - d. 9

Kreuzworträtsel

M

Vertical

2. lucky number in dice
3. 10, 8, 6, 4, ..., 0, −2
4. April, June and September have a total of ... days.
5. 10 centuries = ... years
9. sechs ... zwei = acht
10. He started first grade when he was ... years old.
12. mathematical word for minus
13. one dozen
15. two numbers after "neun"
17. Reverse this number and it's still the same.
18. square root of nine
20. "Ein ..." asks many foolish questions.

Horizontal

1. Self multiplied, it is unchanged.
3. 1800 ÷ 9 = ...
6. how many
7. square of three
8. Its square is twenty-five.
11. After "neunzehn" comes ....
14. "geteilt ..."
16. word for this sign: ×
18. two and one half dozen = ... (ß = ss)
19. ¼ of 60
21. square of two or square root of sixteen
22. "Wie viel...?"
23. ⅖ of 100

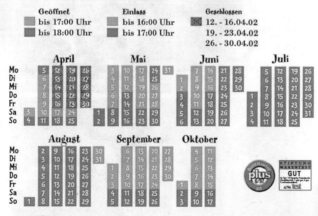

5

Deutschland (Germany)

Berlin, the capital of Germany, is a publishing and fashion center and home of the Berlin Philharmonic Orchestra and the Dahlem Museum. Berlin is also the site of the Brandenburg Gate and an important cultural center. It is the home of the Brecht Ensemble Theater and the Pergamon Museum with its collection of Classical Greek artifacts.

Bonn, a small city on the Rhine River, is the birthplace of the composer Ludwig van Beethoven.

Köln ("colonia"), a former Roman colony, is an industrial city known for its Gothic cathedral, perfume, "4711-Kölnisch Wasser," and for its annual carnival parade.

Hamburg is the largest seaport of Germany and a major industrial center. It is the site of Hagenbeck's Zoo and many beautiful parks.

München, the site of the *Oktoberfest,* is a major cultural center with art galleries and orchestras.

Leipzig, an industrial and cultural city on the Weiße Elster and the Pleiße Rivers, is a publishing and fur center. It hosts the biannual trade fair *(Leipziger Messe)* and is the home of the Gewandhaus Orchestra and the Church of St. Thomas with its famous Boys' Choir.

Dresden, called the "Florence of the North" because of its many artworks, is an important manufacturing and industrial center. It is known for its *Dresdner Stollen* (Christmas fruit bread) and for its porcelain.

Schweiz (Switzerland)

Bern is the capital of the nation. It is located on the Aare River.

Genf (Geneva) is an international conference center and second home of many international film stars.

Zürich is a famous world banking center.

Switzerland has picturesque resort areas such as the city of Luzern and ski centers such as Gstaad and St. Moritz.

Österreich (Austria)

Wien (Vienna) is the capital city of the nation and a major industrial and cultural center. It is the home of the Vienna Boys' Choir and the Spanish Riding School with its white Lippizan stallions. It is a center of music with opera houses and orchestras.

Salzburg, the birthplace of the composer Wolfgang Amadeus Mozart, is a city that derives its name from a castle and a salt mine. The filming of the motion picture *Sound of Music* took place here.

"Nordsee" stands for North Sea, but "Ostsee" is called Baltic Sea, not East Sea.

Deutschland   Schweiz   Österreich

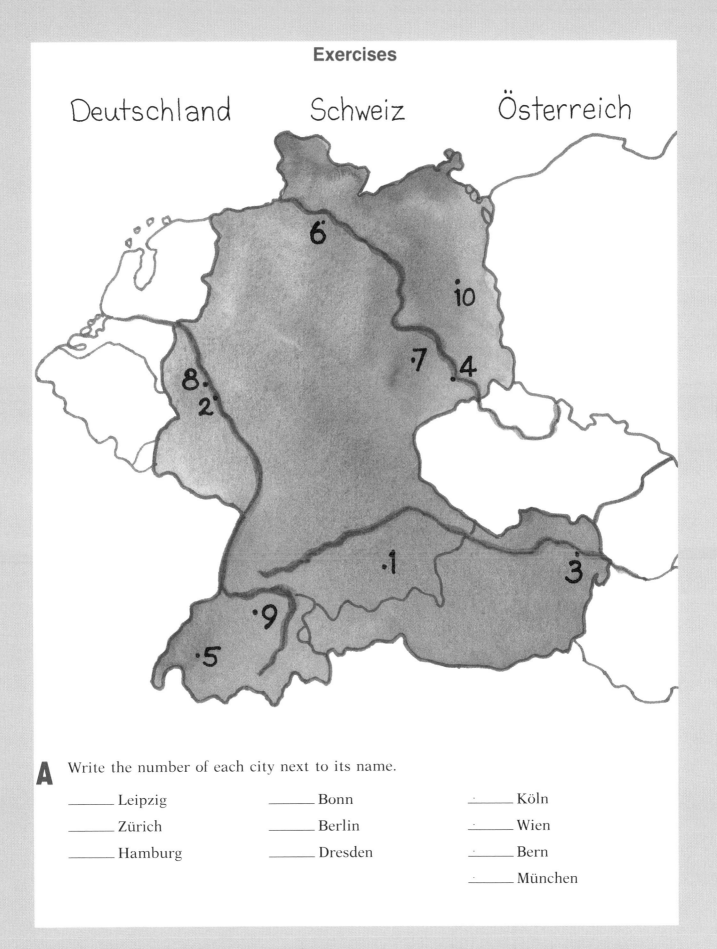

A Write the number of each city next to its name.

_____ Leipzig   _____ Bonn   _____ Köln

_____ Zürich   _____ Berlin   _____ Wien

_____ Hamburg   _____ Dresden   _____ Bern

                                                 _____ München

B   Identify the cities described in the information below.

1. home of the Spanish Riding School with its white Lippizan stallions

   _____

2. site of the annual "Oktoberfest"

   _____

3. site of the Brandenburg Gate

   _____

4. city noted for perfumes and pleasant fragrances

   _____

5. site of a famous fair twice a year

   _____

6. capital of Switzerland

   _____

7. birthplace of Mozart

   _____

8. site of the Dahlem Museum

   _____

9. city noted for art treasures

   _____

10. largest seaport of Germany

   _____

C   After studying the maps carefully, find the following items.

1. one river that forms, in part, the boundary of two countries

   _____

2. one large mountain range which extends over several countries

   _____

3. one river which flows through the cities of Dresden and Hamburg

   _____

4. one lake on the border of two countries

   _____

D Match column B with column A.

	A		**B**
1.	Bonn	_____	a. east of München, close to the German border
2.	Berlin	_____	b. on the southern end of the Elbe
3.	Leipzig	_____	c. on the Donau
4.	Salzburg	_____	d. near the mouth of the Elbe
5.	Wien	_____	e. on the Weiße Elster and Pleiße
6.	Bern	_____	f. north of Dresden and east of the Elbe
7.	Hamburg	_____	g. on the Rhein
8.	Dresden	_____	h. on the Aare

E Nenne die Stadt, die zu jeder Abbildung passt! *Name the city associated with each picture.*

1. _____

2. _____

3. _____

4. _____

5. _____

F   Wähle die richtige Antwort!

1. Wien is the capital of .....
   a. Germany   b. Liechtenstein   c. Switzerland   d. Austria

2. "Harz" is the name of a ....
   a. mountain range   b. city   c. river   d. sea

3. München is a city in the .... of Germany.
   a. south   b. east   c. north   d. west

4. A country that borders Austria to the west is ....
   a. Germany   b. France   c. Switzerland   d. Italy

5. Hamburg is a seaport on the ....
   a. Rhein   b. Donau   c. Aare   d. Elbe

6. Berlin is located .... of Leipzig.
   a. west   b. north   c. east   d. south

7. Poland lies to the .... of Germany.
   a. west   b. north   c. south   d. east

8. Leipzig is a ....
   a. city   b. river   c. country   d. lake

9. The Alps are a ....
   a. country   b. lake   c. mountain range   d. river

10. In Germany, the lowlands are located in the ....
    a. south   b. north   c. east   d. west

G   Write in each blank space the answer that makes each statement geographically correct.

Located in northern Europe, Germany has a variety of geographical features. It has two seacoasts, one on the Nordsee or 1._____ and the other on the Ostsee or 2._____. Crossed by canals and dotted with many small lakes, the northern lowlands cover about one-third of the country. Rolling hills and small mountain ranges cover the remaining two-thirds. One centrally located range is the 3._____.

Germany has many neighbors. Far to the north is 4._____ and to the east are 5._____ and 6._____. To the south are two German-speaking nations, 7._____ and 8._____. To the west are 9._____, 10._____, 11._____ and 12._____. Although the nearby principality of 13._____ does not share a border with Germany, it is a close neighbor and shares the language.

In the German-speaking area of Europe there are two capitals which begin with the letter "B." They are 14._____ and 15._____. Two other capitals begin with "V": 16._____ and 17._____ (or "Wien" in German).

The huge mountain range called the 18._____ boasts magnificent scenery, including glaciers and mountain lakes. However, there is always the possibility of avalanches, especially in the spring. Mountain climbing and skiing are popular pastimes in the Alpine countries. Two well-known ski resorts are 19._____ and 20._____.

H Imagine that you must plan an itinerary (list of sightseeing places) for two groups of American tourists. The first group would like to see cultural sites (i.e., things or places pertaining to music, art, or theater). The second group would like to see athletic events and visit recreational resorts. Which places would you suggest for each group and why?

Group 1

_____

_____

_____

_____

_____

_____

Group 2

_____

_____

_____

_____

_____

_____

Maze

Marianne and Michael are ready to travel. Trace their vacation route to find out where they will be spending the summer. Name their destination in the space provided. List the places they will visit while en route.

Places they'll visit:

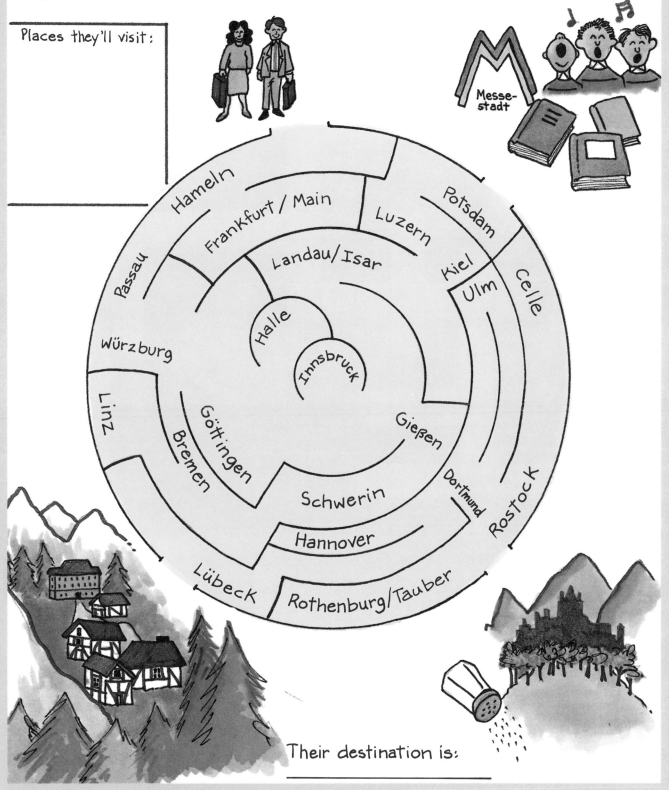

Messe-stadt

Hameln
Frankfurt / Main
Potsdam
Luzern
Passau
Landau / Isar
Kiel
Ulm
Celle
Würzburg
Halle
Innsbruck
Linz
Göttingen
Gießen
Bremen
Dortmund
Schwerin
Rostock
Hannover
Lübeck
Rothenburg / Tauber

Their destination is:

Kreuzworträtsel

J

Vertical

1. capital city on the Danube (German spelling)
3. site of the Gewandhaus Orchestra
5. long navigable river
7. mountain range
8. birthplace of Mozart

Horizontal

2. another long navigable river (German spelling)
4. "Florence of the North"
6. banking center of Switzerland
9. seaport and industrial center
10. city on the Rhine
11. capital city of Germany

Holzfeld

Prämiertes Dorf

RHEINLAND-PFALZ

Westerhever Leuchtturm

① Autobahnabfahrt Reichenbach
② Autobahnabfahrt Zwickau West

HOUSE
Haus

Monika: Wo wohnst du?	Where do you live?
Andreas: Ich wohne in einem Haus in Dresden.	I live in a house in Dresden.
Stefan: Wo ist der Garten?	Where is the garden?
Gisela: Der Garten ist da drüben.	The garden is over there.
Bettina: Wo sind die Garagen?	Where are the garages?
Kurt: Sie sind hinter dem Garten.	They are behind the garden.
Karin: Wie viele Zimmer gibt es in deinem Haus?	How many rooms are there in your house?
Dieter: Es gibt neun Zimmer.	There are nine rooms.

die Zimmer im Haus

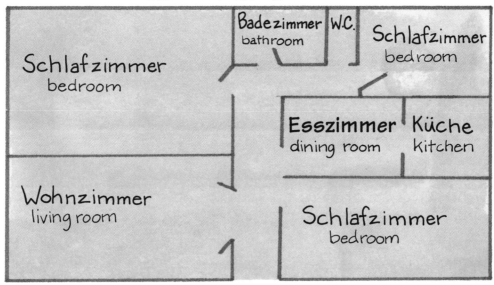

 Wenn die Katze aus dem Haus ist, tanzen die Mäuse.

When the cat's away, the mice will play.

Villa

Einfamilienhaus

Mietshaus

Wohnung

Wohnwagen

Hütte

Zelt

Exercises

A Schreib das deutsche Wort für jedes Zimmer!

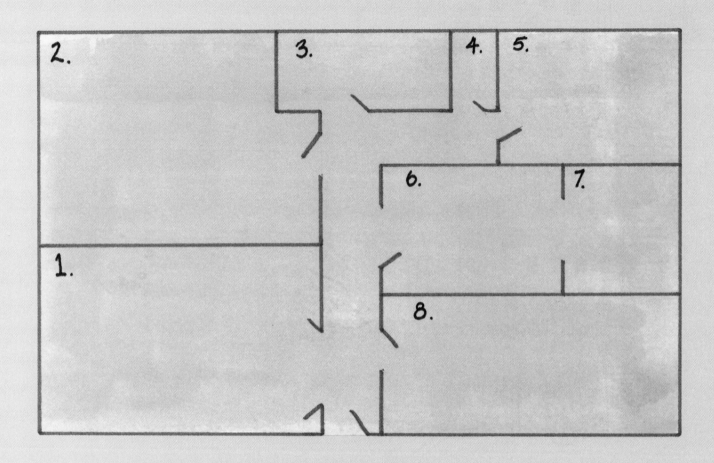

B Ergänze die Sätze!

1. Ich <u>koche</u> in der _____.
   (to cook)

2. Ich <u>schlafe</u> in dem _____.
   (to sleep)

3. Ich <u>esse</u> in dem _____.
   (to eat)

4. Ich <u>bade</u> in dem _____.
   (to bathe)

5. Ich <u>wohne</u> in dem _____.
   (to live)

6. Ich <u>spiele</u> in dem _____.
   (to play)

C   Wähle das richtige Zimmer!

1. Wohnzimmer   (bathroom   kitchen   living room)
2. Schlafzimmer   (dining room   bedroom   bathroom)
3. Badezimmer   (living room   bathroom   bedroom)
4. Esszimmer   (dining room   kitchen   living room)
5. Küche   (bedroom   living room   kitchen)

D   In which room would you find a...(Auf Deutsch, bitte.)

1. bed? _____

2. stove? _____

3. sofa? _____

4. toothbrush? _____

5. dining table? _____

E   Complete each sentence with the appropriate German word.

1. If you went camping, you would sleep in a

_____.

2. If you lived in an apartment, you would call it a

_____.

3. If you lived in a single house, you would call it an

_____.

4. If you lived in a large beautiful house, you would call it a

_____.

5. If you found a rough shelter in the woods, you would call it a

_____.

6. If you slept in a mobile residence, you would call it a

_____.

F   Schreib die Wörter richtig! *Unscramble the words.*

1. ELTZ _____

2. MEIMZR _____

3. ÜKECH _____

4. ASHU _____

5. TRAGEN _____

HAUS   FAMILIE   LIEBE

G Lies den Absatz. Wähle die richtigen Antworten!

Hier ist mein Haus. Es ist schön. Meine Familie wohnt hier. Ich liebe meine Familie und mein Haus. Das Haus hat sieben Zimmer. Hinter dem Haus ist der Garten.

1. Meine Familie wohnt. . . .
    a. Zimmer   c. Liebe
    b. in einem Haus   d. Garten

2. Mein Haus ist. . . .
    a. neu   c. schön
    b. alt   d. klein

3. Mein Haus hat. . .Zimmer.
    a. fünf   c. sieben
    b. sechs   d. acht

4. Der Garten ist hinter dem. . . .
    a. Haus   c. Zimmer
    b. Familie   d. Garten

Kreuzworträtsel

H

Vertical

1. place to bathe
2. place to live
3. located in a "Mietshaus"
4. simple wooden building
6. found in all residences
7. large luxurious house

Horizontal

3. house on wheels
5. place to prepare meals
6. canvas shelter
8. "...haus," kind of house
9. place to play or to plant flowers

FAMILY
Familie

Markus: Wer ist das?
Heidi: Das ist mein <u>Bruder</u>.

Who is that?
That's my <u>brother</u>.

Rudi: Wer sind die Kinder?
Stefan: Sie sind meine <u>Enkelkinder.</u>

Who are the children?
They are my <u>grandchildren</u>.

Sabine: Sind das deine <u>Eltern</u>?
Evelyn: Ja, meine <u>Mutter</u> heißt Judith und mein <u>Vater</u> heißt Josef.

Are they your <u>parents</u>?
Yes, my <u>mother's</u> name is Judith and my <u>father's</u> name is Josef.

Christl: Renate und Brigitte sind <u>Schwestern</u> nicht wahr?
Werner: Ja, und sie sind auch meine <u>Kusinen</u>.

Renate and Brigitte are <u>sisters</u>, aren't they?
Yes, and they are also my <u>cousins</u>.

Vergiss nicht:
Familientreffen-Gäste:

• Großvater, Großmutter
• Tante Rosalinda und ihr Mann
• Kusine Marille
• Cousin Lorenz
• meine Schwester und ihre Kinder
• Andreas und seine Frau
• Gisela und das Baby

Don't forget:
Family Reunion Guests:

• grandfather, grandmother
• Aunt Rosalinda and her husband
• Cousin Marille
• Cousin Lorenz
• my sister and her children
• Andreas and his wife
• Gisela and the baby

Hanni: Wo sind deine Verwandten?
Franz: Meine <u>Großeltern</u> sind drinnen und meine <u>Tanten</u> und <u>Onkel</u> sind im Garten.

Where are your relatives?
My <u>grandparents</u> are inside and my <u>aunts</u> and <u>uncles</u> are in the garden.

Lynnie: Sind deine <u>Paten</u> hier?
Susanne: Ja, sicher. Meine <u>Patin</u> spricht gerade mit meinen Tanten. Mein Pate ist auf der Terrasse.

Are your <u>godparents</u> here?
Yes, of course. My <u>godmother</u> is speaking with my aunts. My <u>godfather</u> is on the terrace.

Eberhard: Wie heißen dein <u>Neffe</u> und deine <u>Nichte</u>?
Hans: Mein Neffe heißt Axel und meine Nichte heißt Michaela.

What are the names of your <u>nephew</u> and your <u>niece</u>?
My nephew's name is Arel and my niece's name is Michaela.

Lars: Bist du ihr einziger <u>Onkel</u>?
Peter: Nein, auch Michael ist ihr Onkel.

Are you their only uncle?
No, Michael is also their uncle.

 Kinder und Narren sprechen die Wahrheit.

Children and fools speak the truth.

das Mädchen — girl

das Kind — child

der Junge — boy

die Tochter — daughter

der Sohn — son

die Enkelin — granddaughter

der Enkel — grandson

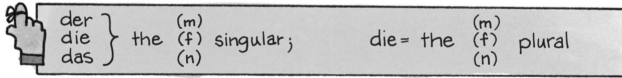

der
die } the (m) (f) (n) singular;   die = the (m) (f) (n) plural

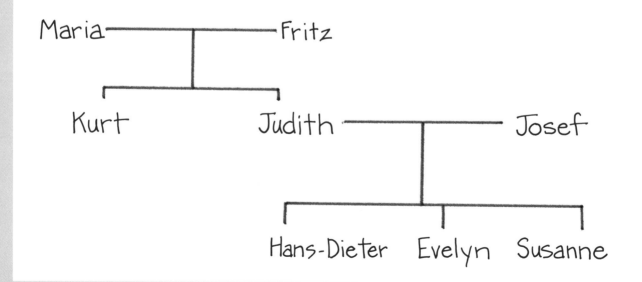

Maria ———————— Fritz

Kurt   Judith ———————— Josef

Hans-Dieter   Evelyn   Susanne

Exercises

A Indicate Susanne's relationship to each family member listed.

Susanne ist die
1. _____Schwester_____ von Evelyn.
2. _____ von Hans-Dieter.
3. _____ von Josef.
4. _____ von Maria.
5. _____ von Kurt.
6. _____ von Fritz.
7. _____ von Judith.

B Tu nun das Gleiche für Judith und Fritz! *Now do the same for Judith and Fritz.*

Judith ist die
1. _____ von Susanne, Hans-Dieter und Evelyn.
2. _____ von Josef.
3. _____ von Kurt.
4. _____ von Fritz und Maria.

Fritz ist der
1. _____ von Maria.
2. _____ von Judith und Kurt.
3. _____ von Hans-Dieter, Evelyn und Susanne.

C Wer ist das? *Who is that?* (Auf deutsch, bitte.)

1. "Bruder" of my "Vater" _____

2. "Sohn" of my "Tante" _____

3. "Mutter" of my "Mutter" _____

4. "Tochter" of my "Onkel" _____

5. "Sohn" of my "Eltern" _____

D Wer bin ich? *Who am I?* (Auf deutsch, bitte.)

1. I am your cousin's mother.
   In other words, I am your _____.
2. I am your father's brother.
   In other words, I am your _____.
3. I am your male sibling.
   In other words, I am your _____.
4. I am your offspring.
   In other words, I am your _____.

E Wähle die richtige Antwort!

1. Wo ist das Kind?
    a. on the bench
    b. in the playpen
    c. in the foreground

2. Wo sind die Großeltern?
    a. on the bench
    b. in the playpen
    c. in the foreground

3. Wo sind die Eltern?
    a. on the bench
    b. in the playpen
    c. in the foreground

F Schreib auf englisch!

1. Wer ist das? _____

2. Wer singt? _____

3. Wer ist der Mann? _____

4. Wer kommt zu der Party? _____

G Ergänze auf Deutsch!

1. Wer ist der Junge? (son)
    Der Junge ist mein _____.

2. Wer ist die Frau? (mother)
    Die Frau ist meine _____.

3. Wer ist das Mädchen? (niece)
    Das Mädchen ist meine _____.

H Lies den Absatz. Schreib den Absatz auf Englisch! *Read the paragraph. Write it in English.*

Meine Familie

Ich habe eine kleine Familie. Mein Vater ist sechsunddreißig Jahre alt. Meine Mutter ist siebenunddreißig Jahre alt. Meine Schwester heißt Ingrid und sie ist acht. Mein Bruder heißt Hans und er ist fünf. Ich heiße Patricia. Meine Familie wohnt in Lübeck und meine Großeltern wohnen in Berlin.

> wohnen – to live, reside

_____

_____

_____

_____

_____

_____

frohe Weihnachten
und ein gutes
neues Jahr

Unsere kleine
Christina Laura
wurde am 23. 10. 2002 geboren
um 15.45 Uhr
Gewicht: 3370 Gramm
Größe: 51 cm

In dankbarer Freude
die glücklichen Eltern

Wolfgang und Andrea Kern geb. Heiner
Landau-Queichheim   Rohrbach

Die fröhliche Guten-Tag-Anzeige

Lieber Opa Siggi,

60 Jahre wirst du heute
und es gratulieren viele Leute.
Es grüßen dich die deinen,
ganz besonders deine Kleinen.
Wir wünschen dir ein langes Leben,
viel Gesundheit, Glück und Gottes Segen.
Hoch, hoch soll unser Opa leben.

Helena, Lilith und Marlin

Liebe Anja!

Zu Deinem **30. Geburtstag**

wünschen wir dir
alles Liebe, Gute, Glück
und Gesundheit

Deine Schätze
Roger + Sophia

Jonas
hat ein Schwesterchen bekommen
Ann-Kristin
• 30. 11. 2002 • 3 640 g • 52 cm
Wir freuen uns riesig,
dass sie gesund und munter bei uns ist.
Martin und Reinhilde Luhme
Gevelinghausen

Ein besonderer Dank gilt der Praxis Dr. Nabil Bushnaq,
Hebamme Martina Cruse, Dr. Oldeowa, Station 6 des
St.-Walburga-Krankenhauses Meschede.

Das Fest der
Goldenen Hochzeit
feiern heute
Isabell & Helmut Gehrlein
dazu gratulieren wir euch recht herzlich und
wünschen für die Zukunft alles erdenklich Gute
Eure Kinder: Bernadette, Berthold,
Natalie, Ina und Christian
Neupotz, 4. November 2002

8 OCCUPATIONS
Berufe

Was ist dein Beruf?
Ich bin Schauspieler.

Was machst du?
Ich bin Schauspielerin.

What is your occupation?
I am an actor.

What do you do? (for a living)
I am an actress.

der Arzt	m	} physician
die Ärztin	f	
der Koch	m	} cook
die Köchin	f	
der Geschäftsmann	m	} businessman
die Geschäftsfrau	f	} businesswoman

Acme Arbeitsvermittlung
sucht:

Tischler, -in   Künstler, -in
Musiker, -in   Lehrer, -in
Mechaniker, -in Elektriker, -in
Landwirt, -in   Briefträger, -in
Klempner, -in   Krankenpfleger, -in

Arbeitstellen garantiert.
Tel. 12-59-43

Acme Employment Agency
is looking for:

carpenter   artist
musician   teacher
mechanic   electrician
farmer   letter carrier
plumber   nurse

Work guaranteed.
Tel. 12-59-43

 Jeder ist seines
Glückes Schmied.

One forges one's own
destiny.

Exercises

A Number in order the professions or trades as your teacher recites them.

die Ärztin _____   der Lehrer _____

der Geschäftsmann _____   die Mechanikerin _____

die Künstlerin _____   der Koch _____

der Landwirt _____   der Klempner _____

die Briefträgerin _____   die Musikerin _____

B Wer arbeitet hier? *Who works here?*

1. stage _____

2. dairy farm _____

3. post office _____

4. recording studio _____

5. studio _____

6. hospital _____

7. kitchen _____

8. wood shop _____

9. school _____

10. garage _____

C Schreib die Wörter richtig.

1. RELRHE _____

2. TIRDWALN _____

3. ITZÄRN _____

4. INCHÖK _____

5. PLNERKEM _____

D Wie heißt das auf Englisch? *Write the sentences in English. Look first, then take a good guess.*

1. Mein Vater ist Mechaniker.

   _____

2. Er repariert Autos.

   _____

3. Meine Mutter ist Sekretärin.

   _____

4. Sie tippt Briefe.

   _____

5. Mein Onkel ist Lehrer.

   _____

6. Er lehrt.

   _____

7. Meine Tante ist Briefträgerin.

   _____

8. Sie bringt Briefe.

   _____

E Guess who...(Auf Deutsch, bitte.)

1. Der _____ instructs students

2. Die _____ is in charge of the (medical) operation.

3. Der _____ checks for faulty wiring.

4. Die _____ installs water pipes.

5. Der _____ paints portraits.

6. Die _____ cooks food.

7. Der _____ manages a company.

8. Die _____ milks cows.

9. Der _____ delivers mail.

10. Die _____ plays in a symphony orchestra.

F   Schreib einen Beruf zu jeder Abbildung!

1. _____

2. _____

3. _____

4. _____

5. _____

Was gibt's zu essen ?
Es gibt Salat und Suppe.

What is there to eat?
There is salad and soup.

Hast du Hunger?
Ja. Ich habe Hunger.

Are you hungry?
Yes. I'm hungry.

Hast du Durst ?
Nein. Ich habe keinen Durst.

Are you thirsty?
No. I'm not thirsty.

Patricks Lebensmittel
Getränke — Verkauf

Kaffee „Karib" (½ Kg) €	5,—
Tee (¼ Kg)	3,—
Milch (1 Liter)	2,—
Schokoladenpulver	1,50
Mineralwasser (2 Liter)	1,—
Fruchtsaft (Dose)	1,50

Patrick's Grocery
Beverage — Sale

"Caribe" coffee (½ Kg) €	5.00
tea (¼ Kg)	3.00
milk (1 liter)	2.00
chocolate powder mix	1.50
mineral water (2 liters)	1.00
fruit juice (can)	1.50

Hannis Ecke
Ländliche Küche

Tagesgericht — Freitag

Menü
- Klare Hühnersuppe
- Kalbsbraten
  - grüne Bohnen
  - Röstkartoffeln
  - gemischter Salat
- Nachtisch   SF 16,—

Bei uns schmeckt's immer!

Hanni's Corner
Regional Food

Menu of the day — Friday

Menu
- chicken broth
- roast veal
  - green beans
  - fried potatoes
  - mixed salad
- dessert   SF 16.—

Always tasty here!

 Viele Köche verderben den Brei.

Too many cooks spoil the stew.

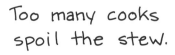

Apfelsine

Birne

Ananas

Apfel

Banane

OBST

breakfast = Frühstück
lunch or midday
main meal = Mittagessen
supper (light)
supper (main meal) = Abendessen

Einkaufsliste   Shopping List

Spinat — spinach
Kuchen — cake
Steak — steak
Brot — bread
Kekse — cookies
Kartoffeln — potatoes
Tomaten — tomatoes
Hähnchen — chicken
Käse — cheese
Puddingpulver — instant pudding
Eis — ice cream

 Guten Appetit! — A wish on the part of a friend or host that all the guests may enjoy the meal and eat heartily.

der Pfeffer
pepper

das Salz
salt

die Vase
vase

die Butter
butter

das Glas
glass

die Tasse
cup

die Untertasse
saucer

die Serviette
napkin

der Teller
plate

der Zucker
sugar

die Gabel
fork

das Messer
knife

der Teelöffel
teaspoon

die Tischdecke
tablecloth

der Löffel
spoon

der Tisch
table

Specialties of Germany, Austria and Switzerland

Wiener Schnitzel – breaded and fried veal cutlets; specialty of Vienna, Austria

Sauerbraten – pot roast of marinated beef served with a sour cream gravy and accompanied by red cabbage and potato pancakes

Königsberger Klopse – meatballs flavored with a sauce of cloves, peppercorns, capers and lemon juice and served with buttered noodles; specialty of Königsberg in the former coastal territory of East Prussia

Kartoffelpuffer – potato pancakes prepared with eggs, onion and parsley and fried until golden brown and crispy, served as a main or side dish

Spätzle – noodles made of a flour and egg mixture dropped by the spoon into boiling water and served with butter; specialty of southwestern Germany

Klöße or *Knödel* – dumplings of many varieties used in soups, as side dishes or even as desserts

Lebkuchen – cakes of honey and spices often shaped into hearts and decorated with sayings and proverbs; specialty of Nuremberg (Nürnberg)

Schwarzwälder Kirschtorte – Black Forest Cherry Cake – layer cake with whipped cream, cherry flavored liqueur, cherries and chocolate; specialty of southwestern Germany

Raclette – melted cheese served with boiled potatoes; simple specialty of Switzerland

Exercises

A Schreib das deutsche Wort für jedes Objekt!

1. _____

2. _____

3. _____

4. _____

5. _____

6. _____

B Ergänze jeden Satz!

1. Potato pancakes are often served with _____.

2. To make "Raclette" one needs to melt _____.

3. "Wiener Schnitzel" is a specialty of _____.

4. A dessert made with honey is _____.

5. The meat of "Sauerbraten" is _____

C Using your food vocabulary list, write three food items for each of the following categories.

meat

1. _____

2. _____

3. _____

vegetables

1. _____

2. _____

3. _____

dairy products

1. _____

2. _____

3. _____

beverages

1. _____

2. _____

3. _____

fruits

1. _____

2. _____

3. _____

desserts

1. _____

2. _____

3. _____

D Answer either 1 or 2 *and* 3 or 4.

1. You are opening a restaurant in Germany. From your food list prepare a menu for lunch and dinner. At least three dishes for each meal should be offered. Specialty dishes may be used.

2. Prepare a poster from magazine pictures. Show a balanced breakfast and a balanced dinner. Label each food with its German name.

3. Prepare 15 different flashcards with a picture of a food item on one side and its German name on the other.

4. List in German 15 words which name a food. Then scramble each word. These can be used in classroom games.
   Example: BIRNE = RIBEN
             EIS = SIE

Kreuzworträtsel

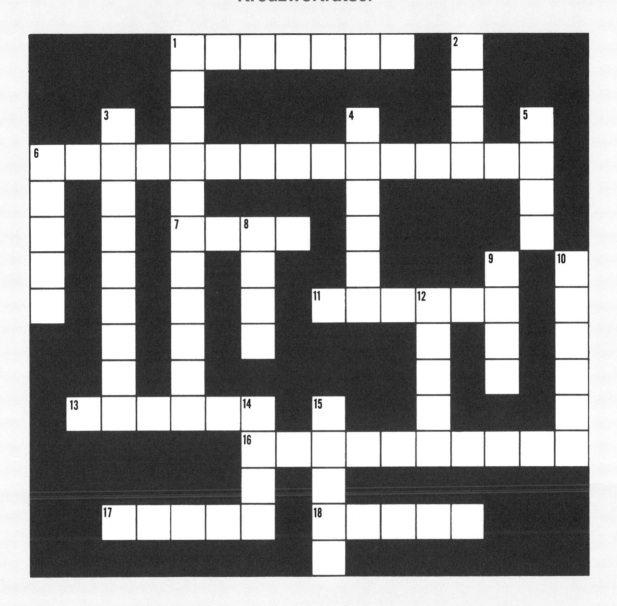

E

Vertical

1. marinated pot roast
2. adds zest to many foods
3. Nuremberg honey cakes
4. other name for "Klöße"
5. One drinks from this.
6. general name for sausage
8. apples, pears, plums
9. Dishes are selected from this.
10. cake
12. served before the main dish
14. orange, tomato, grapefruit
15. often served with milk or tea

Horizontal

1. drop noodles
6. Viennese veal cutlet
7. made from dough for sandwiches
11. name for dumplings (ß = ss)
13. famous Hawaiian fruit
16. evening meal
17. quenched by "Wasser"
18. tossed, fruit, chef's

ANHALTISCHE KARTOFFELSUPPE

1,5 Liter kräftige Rinderbrühe
450 gr. Kartoffelwürfel roh
150 gr. frischen Lauch, Sellerie, Möhren
100 gr. Zwiebeln
100 gr. Speck
Salz, Pfeffer, Majoran, Lorbeerlaub, Piment, feingehackte Liebstöckel
frisch gehackte Gartenkräuter

Die kleingewürfelten Kartoffeln (mehlig kochende Sorte) in einer kräftigen Rinderbrühe kochen. Die Brühe schon mit Lorbeerlaub, wenig Piment, Salz und Pfeffer würzen. Das kleingewürfelte Gemüse später hinzugeben. Den kleingewürfelten Speck in der Pfanne goldgelb auslassen. Die feingewürfelten Zwiebeln dazu geben und glasig anschwitzen. Das Zwiebel-Speckgemisch in den Kartoffeltopf hinzugeben. Die Suppe mit Majoran, Salz, frisch gemahlenen Pfeffer, den feingehackten Liebstöckel abschmecken.

Die Suppe kann verfeinert werden mit frischen Kräutern oder auch Kräutersahne.

Sauerbraten

Zutaten:

1–2 l Wasser

1/4 l Essig

3–4 große Zwiebeln

Salz

Nelken

Pfeffer

Lorbeer

1 kg Rinderschmorbraten

100 g Margarine

100 g Möhren

Sellerie

Petersilie

Tomatenmark

Reibekuchen

ART
Kunst

Three Great Artists
Drei berühmte Künstler

Albrecht Dürer (1471–1528) used his study of Classical art to draw the human form realistically. This Renaissance artist from Nürnberg also used his skills to portray nature exactly. Dürer was equally masterful at wood carving, copper engraving and drawing. His style is Classical, with much attention paid to actual proportion. Like those of other artists of his time, his works frequently used religious themes or reflected his concern about war. *The Young Hare, Saint Anthony* and *The Four Horsemen* are three of his famous works.

Caspar David Friedrich (1774-1840), a North German painter from Greifswald, is an important artist of the Romantic School. He found little need to learn from the Classical masters of Rome, but gathered his inspiration from nature and the beauty of his native countryside. Friedrich was captivated by the contrariness of nature. He realized that nature could be at one time peaceful and at another time violent. He also knew that nature had a charming side and a cruel side. Landscapes and seascapes offered this great artist the means to express this viewpoint. In *Ships in the Harbor of Greifswald*, the viewer might say, the sunrise promises to drive away the gloom and the mystery of night. Or, the viewer might say, the shadows of evening threaten the peacefulness of the ships at anchor. In the *Lone Tree*, the serenity of the vast landscape is disturbed by the sight of a once majestic old tree which has been devastated by lightning.

Ernst Ludwig Kirchner (1880–1938) studied art at the Dresden Technical School. He experimented with both oils and woodcuts and was successful at both. He was convinced that art was being strangled by Romanticism and modern society. To remedy this, he founded a community of artists called the "Bridge" or "Brücke". His group tried to express the frantic pace of modern city life. A good example of this Expressionist art is *Street, Berlin*, painted by Kirchner in 1913.

Meanwhile, in Munich, another Expressionist group called the "Blue Rider" displayed a style characterized by bold heavy outlines, vivid colors and naive features. *The Large Blue Horses* by Franz Marc is a good example of this style of Expressionism.

 Die Kunst ist lang, das Leben kurz. Art is long but life is short.

The Young Hare
(water color, 1502)
by Albrecht Dürer
Kunstverlag M.u.D. Reisser, Wien

Saint Anthony
(copper engraving, 1519)
by Albrecht Dürer
Staatliche Graphische Sammlung, München

The Large Blue Horses
(oil on canvas, 1911)
by Franz Marc

Collection, Walker Art Center, Minneapolis;
Gift of the T.B. Walker Foundation,
Gilbert M. Walker Fund, 1942

Street, Berlin
(oil on canvas, 1913)
by Ernst Ludwig Kirchner
Collection, The Museum of Modern Art, New York Purchase.

Ships in the Harbor of Greifswald
(oil on canvas, before 1810)
by Caspar David Friedrich
Staatliche Museen Preußischer
Kulturbesitz, Nationalgalerie, Berlin (West)

Lone Tree
(oil on canvas, 1823)
by Caspar David Friedrich
Staatliche Museen Preußischer
Kulturbesitz, Nationalgalerie, Berlin (West)

Exercises

A Name the picture which shows

1. a shepherd leaning against a tree. _____

2. a medieval city. _____

3. an animal at rest. _____

4. animals "moving." _____

5. working people. _____

6. well-dressed city people. _____

B Name the German artist whose works reveal:

1. heavy dark outlines _____

2. exact proportions _____

3. peaceful landscapes _____

4. disturbing elements of nature _____

5. bright colors _____

6. real-looking people or animals _____

C Verbinde B mit A!

A	**B**
1. Dresden _____	a. Dürer
2. Classical style painter _____	b. where Kirchner studied
3. Nürnberg _____	c. Friedrich
4. Romantic style painter _____	d. where Friedrich lived
5. Expressionist style painter _____	e. Kirchner
6. Greifswald _____	f. where Dürer lived

D Complete the analogies.

1. *Lone Tree*: _____ = *The Four Horsemen*: Dürer

2. Friedrich: seascapes = _____: city scene

3. Franz Marc: "The Blue Rider" = Kirchner: _____

4. _____: Classical style = Friedrich: Romantic style

5. _____: Kirchner = *Saint Anthony*: Dürer

Verbinde den Namen mit der Abbildung!

Friedrich

Kirchner

Dürer

F Which artist would most likely be...

1. awed by dark storm clouds as they rumble across the sky?

   _____

2. happy to write a manual on realism and proportion in art?

   _____

3. disgusted to see an irritated crowd of people at a bus stop?

   _____

G In your opinion...

1. whose work of art would delight a group of Renaissance scholars? _____

2. whose work of art would appeal to someone who likes bright colors and unusual

   shapes? _____

3. whose work of art would be appreciated by nature-lovers? _____

H Which of the pictures in this unit do you like the best? _____

Who created this masterpiece? _____

State in your own words what the picture is about and why you like it.

_____

_____

_____

_____

_____

I Ergänze die Sätze!

1. Kirchner and Marc were both _____ painters.

2. Friedrich painted many seascapes and _____.

3. Dürer's works are drawn very _____.

Kulturhistorische Museen

1 MUSEE SUISSE
Schweizerisches Landesmuseum
Museumstrasse 2, Telefon 218 65 11
Internet: www.musee-suisse.ch

Sa–Mi 10–20 Uhr
Mo 14–20 Uhr
Do/Fr 10–18 Uhr

**Museum für
schweizerische Kultur,
Kunst und Geschichte**

2 Zunfthaus zur Meisen
Münsterhof 20, Telefon 221 28 07

Di–So 10.30–17 Uhr
Mo geschlossen

**Schweizer Porzellan
und Fayencen**

3 Museum Bärengasse
Bärengasse 20–22
Telefon 211 17 16

Di–So 10.30–17 Uhr

Vernunft und Leidenschaft.
Zürich 1750–1800

* Museum Hermann Haller
Ecke Bellerivestrasse/Höschgasse
Telefon 383 42 47

Mi–So 12–18 Uhr
Mo und Di geschlossen
Eintritt frei

**4 Archäologische
Sammlung**
Rämistrasse 73
8006 Zürich

Di–Fr 13–18 Uhr
Sa und So 11–17 Uhr
Mo geschlossen
Eintritt frei

Assyrische, ägyptische,
griechische und etruski-
sche Antiken

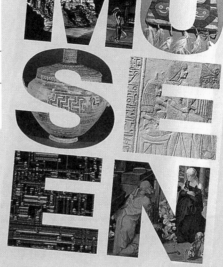

PARTS OF
THE BODY
Körperteile

der Hals

der Kopf

die Schulter

der
Ellenbogen [

die Brust

der Arm

der Bauch

die Hand

das Bein

das Knie

der Fuß

Aus den Augen, aus dem Sinn.   Out of sight, out of mind.

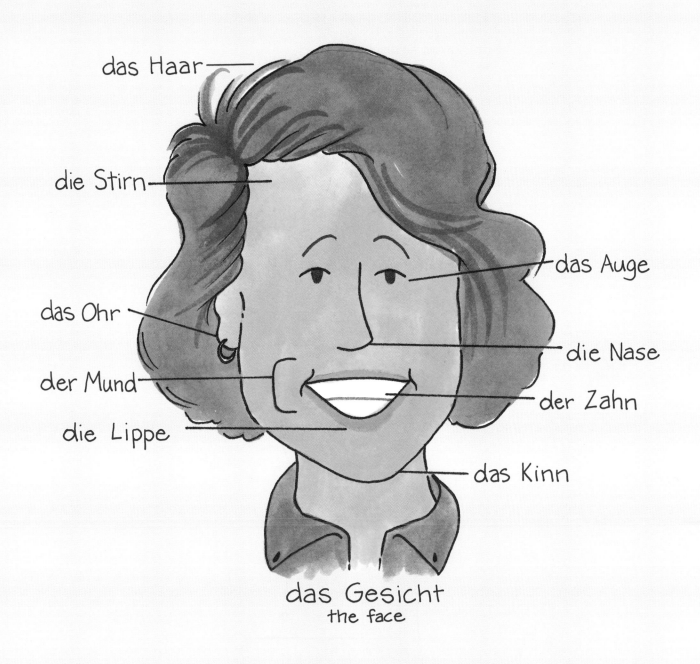

das Haar

die Stirn

das Ohr

der Mund

die Lippe

das Auge

die Nase

der Zahn

das Kinn

das Gesicht
the face

der Finger = the finger
das Gesicht = the face
die Zehe = the toe

die Augen = the eyes
die Lippen = the lips
die Ohren = the ears
die Zähne = the teeth

Exercises

A Label the parts of the body. (Auf Deutsch, bitte.)

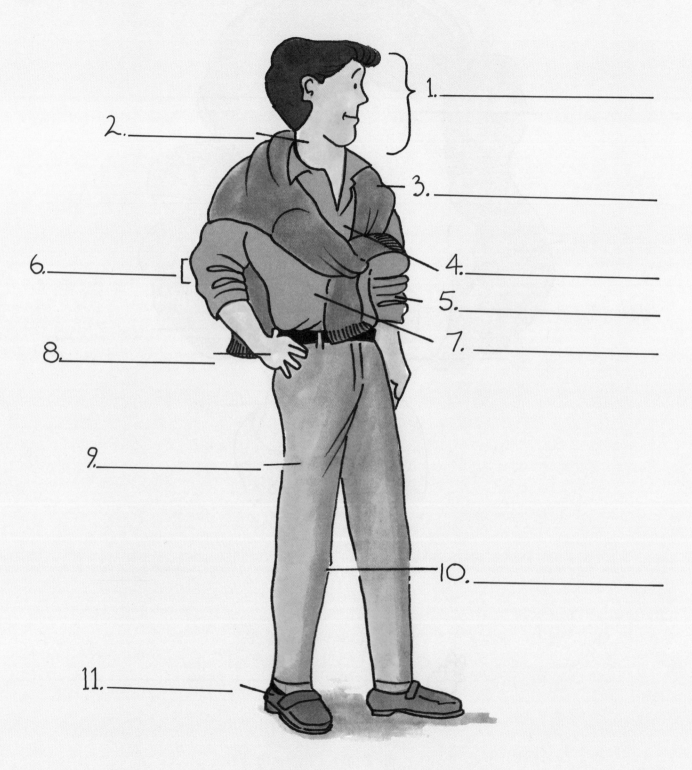

1. _____

2. _____

3. _____

4. _____

5. _____

6. _____

7. _____

8. _____

9. _____

10. _____

11. _____

B Label the parts of the face. (Auf Deutsch, bitte.)

1. _____

2. _____

3. _____

4. _____

5. _____

6. _____

7. _____

8. _____

9. _____

C   Complete the analogies.

1.   das Knie: das Bein = _____: der Arm

2.   _____: der Fuß = der Arm: das Bein

3.   die Finger: _____: die Zehen: der Fuß

D   Ergänze die Sätze auf Deutsch!

1.   A pirate wears a patch over one _____.

2.   The tongue is in the _____.

3.   An _____ is necessary for hearing.

4.   The pen is held in the _____.

5.   _____ are needed to chew food.

6.   The toes are found on the _____.

7.   We used the _____ to smell a rose.

8.   We play a guitar with our _____.

9.   The "funny bone" is located on the _____.

10. If you eat too much, your _____ will hurt.

E   Guess the meaning of the underlined verbs.

1.   Ich *sehe* mit den Augen. _____

2.   Ich *höre* mit den Ohren. _____

3.   Ich *fühle* mit den Fingern. _____

4.   Ich *spreche* mit dem Mund. _____

5.   Ich *rieche* mit der Nase. _____

F Name the part of the body associated with each illustration. (Auf Deutsch, bitte.)

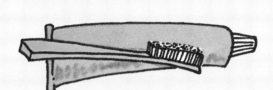

1. _____

2. _____

3. _____

Was für eine Idee!

4. _____

5. _____

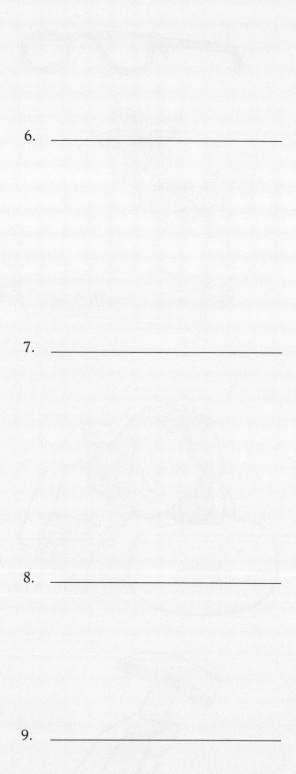

6. _____

7. _____

8. _____

9. _____

10. _____

G Verbinde B mit A.

A	**B**
1. Finger _____	a. smelling
2. Arm _____	b. digesting
3. Bauch _____	c. carrying
4. Nase _____	d. thinking
5. Fuß _____	e. speaking
6. Hand _____	f. listening
7. Auge _____	g. feeling
8. Ohr _____	h. writing
9. Mund _____	i. running
10. Kopf _____	j. seeing

H Lies den Absatz! Wähle die richtigen Antworten!

Ich bin gesund. Ich habe gute Ohren: ich kann gut hören. Ich habe gute Augen: ich kann gut sehen. Ich habe alle Zähne und kann alles essen. Ich habe auch zwei Füße, zwei Beine und zwei Arme. Ich kann gut laufen und schwimmen. Bist du auch gesund?

1. Mein Körper ist...
   - a. Ohren
   - b. hören
   - c. gesund
   - d. zwei

2. Meine Augen sind...
   - a. gut
   - b. auch
   - c. Füße
   - d. sehen

3. Ich esse mit den...
   - a. Ohren
   - b. Zähnen
   - c. Augen
   - d. Beinen

4. Mit den Füßen, Beinen und Armen kann ich...
   - a. essen
   - b. hören
   - c. sehen
   - d. schwimmen

5. Ich bin...
   - a. gesund
   - b. laufen
   - c. ungesund
   - d. essen

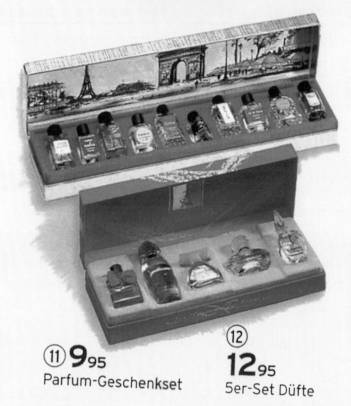

⑪ **9**₉₅
Parfum-Geschenkset

⑫ **12**₉₅
5er-Set Düfte

⑧ **24**₉₅
Profischminke

⑦ je **9**₉₅
Lippenstift-Set

⑨ ab **14**₉₅
„Egyptische Erde"

78

12

CLOTHING
Kleidung

Was hast du an?
Ich habe meine neue Kleidung an.

What are you wearing?
I'm wearing my new clothing.

Lynni
Winterferien
Schweiz—Januar

Lufthansa
Zürich

2 Wollkleider
3 Hüte
1 Schlafanzug
2 Gürtel
3 Taschentücher   3 Hemden
1 Strickjacke   2 Blusen
  Socken
  Handschuhe   Mantel
  Hosen
  Schuhe

Lynni
Winter Vacation
Switzerland—January

Lufthansa
Zürich

2 woolen dresses
3 hats
1 pair of pyjamas
2 belts
3 handkerchiefs   3 shirts
1 cardigan sweater   2 blouses
  socks
  gloves   coat
  pants
  shoes

Moden von Susanne
Oberbekleidung und Unterbekleidung

Bluse

Kleid

Rock

Krawatte

Jacke

Hemd

Pantoffeln

Bademantel

Anzug

Kleider machen Leute.

Clothes make the person.

Exercises

A   Verbinde B mit A.

A	**B**
1. Hüte _____	a. blouse
2. Krawatte _____	b. handkerchief
3. Hemd _____	c. shoes
4. Jacke _____	d. hats
5. Taschentuch _____	e. slippers
6. Bluse _____	f. coat
7. Schuhe _____	g. jacket
8. Pantoffeln _____	h. necktie
9. Mantel _____	i. dress
10. Kleid _____	j. shirt

B   What do you wear...(Auf Deutsch, bitte.)

1. to school? _____

2. to bed? _____

3. to a symphony concert? _____

4. in cold weather? _____

5. in cool weather? _____

C   Complete the analogies.

1. Krawatte: _____ = Gürtel: Hose

2. Bademantel: Schlafanzug = Mantel: _____

3. Handschuhe: Hände = _____: Füße

4. _____: Rock = Hemd: Hose

D Ergänze jeden Satz mit dem Wort für das Bild! *Complete each sentence with the word for the picture.*

1. Ich habe ein _____ an.

2. Ich habe einen _____ an.

3. Ich habe einen _____ an.

4. Ich habe einen _____
   und eine _____ an.

5. Ich habe ein _____
   und eine _____ an.

E Schreib die Wörter auf Englisch!

1. anhaben _____

2. er/sie hat an _____

3. ich habe an _____

4. du hast an _____

F Ergänze auf Englisch!

1. A "Strickjacke" goes (under/over) a shirt. _____

2. "Schuhe" go over my _____ .

3. A "Mantel" is worn when the weather is _____ .

4. A "Bluse" is combined with a _____ to make an outfit.

5. "Pantoffeln" go on my _____ .

G List the required number of items for each category. (Auf Deutsch, bitte.)

outerwear (5)   **accessories (3)**

_____   _____

_____   _____

_____   _____

_____

_____

footwear (3)   **sleepwear (1)**

_____   _____

_____

_____

H Lies den Absatz! Wähle die richtigen Antworten!

Erika geht heute Abend mit ihrer Familie ins Konzert. Sie hat ein schönes Kleid an. Da es kalt ist, hat sie auch einen Mantel und Handschuhe an.

1. Wohin (where to) geht Erika heute Abend?
   a. mit ihrer Familie
   b. Erika
   c. ins Konzert

2. Was hat Erika an?
   a. ein Kleid
   b. eine Hose
   c. einen Schlafanzug

3. Wie ist das Wetter? (weather)
   a. kalt
   b. warm
   c. kühl

4. Was hat Erika über (over) dem Kleid an?
   a. Handschuhe
   b. einen Mantel
   c. ein Kleid

Kreuzworträtsel

Vertical

1. slacks, trousers, pants
2. easily slipped on your feet
3. ...: Rock = Hemd: Hose
4. to wear when it's cold or raining
5. woman: ... = man: Anzug
6. worn on feet outdoors
8. handwarmers
11. worn during cold weather, shorter than coat
13. belts

Horizontal

1. worn on heads
7. put on feet before shoes go on
9. small cloth accessory
10. tie goes on top of...
12. clothing
14. business, leisure, three-piece
15. flared, straight, dirndl
16. must always be worn with a dress shirt

Sympatex Jacke
Kapuze im Kragen

EUR **119.**⁹⁰

Nylon Oberstoff

① ab **24**⁹⁵ Kurz-Pullover

③ ab **39**⁹⁵ Kapuzen-Blazer

④ ab **19**⁹⁵ Top

② ab **29**⁹⁵ Sportliche Hose

⑤ ab **29**⁹⁵ Langer Rock

Umfangreiche Baby-Mode

ab Gr. 50 - Gr. 110
in **chicen Dessins**
und **Formen**

13

TIME
AND COLORS
Zeit und Farben

Wie viel Uhr ist es?
Um wie viel Uhr...?

Es ist halb zwei.

Es ist Viertel vor zehn.

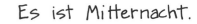

Es ist drei Uhr.

Es ist Mittag.

Es ist Viertel nach sieben.

Es ist Mitternacht.

Es ist fünf nach zwei.

Es ist fünf vor zwölf.

Transportation in Europe operates on official
time, which has a twenty-four hour basis. Official
time is often used by schools, radio and television
stations, theaters and movie theaters.

Zeit ist Geld.

What time is it?
At what time...?

Time is money.

Welche Farbe hat...? What color is...?
Es ist... It is...
Welche Farben haben...? What color are...?
Sie sind... They are...

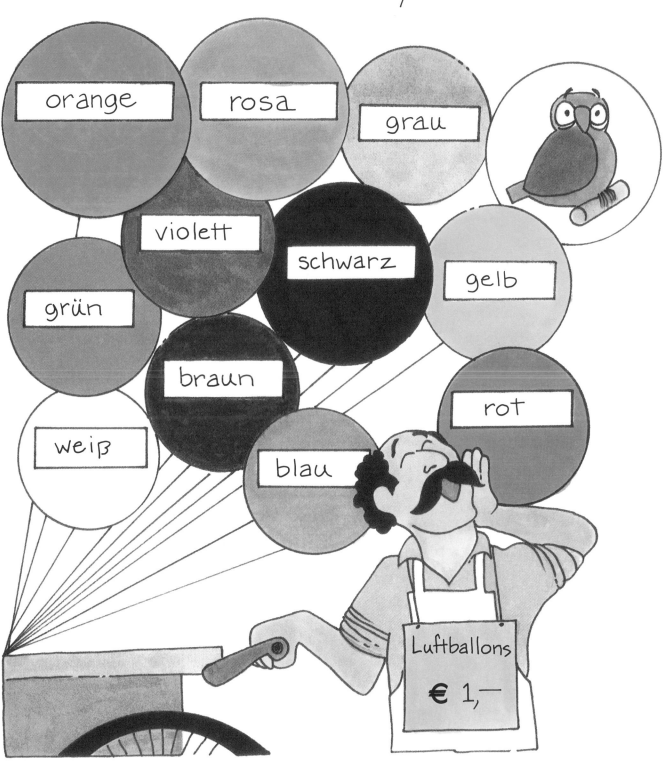

A Listen as your teacher indicates a time. Find the clock which expresses that time. Mark the clock expressing the time said first, number one. Mark the clock expressing the time said next, number two. Continue numbering until all eight clocks are found and marked.

_____   _____   _____   _____

_____   _____   _____   _____

B Ergänze die Sätze auf Deutsch!

1. If the sky is very cloudy, it appears to be _____.

2. If the sky is clear and the sun is shining, the sky is _____.

3. A ripe banana is _____.

4. A leaf in the summer is _____.

5. A piece of coal is _____.

6. A pastel shade of red is _____.

7. A combination of red and yellow is _____.

8. A marshmallow is _____.

9. The color of strawberry is _____.

10. A piece of chocolate is _____.

C Schreib auf Deutsch!

1. at four o'clock _____

2. It's half past nine. _____

3. at 12:45 _____

4. It's 10:00. _____

5. at eighteen minutes after two _____

D Welche Farben haben die Objekte?

A	**B**
1. hearts and tomatoes _____	a. grau
2. frogs and grass _____	b. blau
3. lemons and corn _____	c. grün
4. elephants and rain clouds _____	d. rot
5. forget-me-nots and robins' eggs _____	e. gelb

E Lies den Absatz! Wähle die richtigen Antworten!

   Karin und Rolf gehen heute Abend ins Konzert. Das Orchester heißt die Berliner Philharmonie. Karin hat ein gelbes Kleid an. Rolfs Anzug ist schwarz, sein Hemd ist rosa und seine Krawatte ist grau und rosa. Die Musik beginnt um 20.00 Uhr. Es ist erst 18.00 Uhr. Die jungen Leute haben zwei Stunden Zeit, bis das Konzert beginnt.

heute Abend = this evening	Stunden = hours
jetzt = now	bis = until
die…Leute = the…people	

1. Was ist der Name des Orchesters?
   a. Karin und Rolf   c. Musik
   b. Berliner Philharmonie   d. Konzert

2. Welche Farbe hat Karins Kleid?
   a. rosa   c. schwarz
   b. weiß   d. gelb

3. Passt Rolfs Krawatte zu seinem Anzug? (Passt = Does…match)
   a. ja   b. nein

4. Wie viel Uhr ist es jetzt?
   a. 16.00 Uhr   c. 20.00 Uhr
   b. 18.00 Uhr   d. 22.00 Uhr

5. Um wie viel Uhr beginnt das Konzert?
   a. jetzt   c. um 20.00 Uhr
   b. heute Abend   d. um 18.00 Uhr

Es ist 3 Uhr.

Color the clock according to the directions.

1. Color the "Augen" BRAUN.
2. Color the "Lippen" ROT.
3. Color the "Nase" BLAU.
4. Color the "Haar" VIOLETT
5. Color the "Gesicht" GRAU.
6. Color the "Füße" ROSA.

7. Color the "fünf" GRÜN.
8. Color the "zehn" ORANGE.
9. Color the "elf" SCHWARZ.
10. Color the U GELB.
11. Color the E BLAU.
12. Color the t WEISS.

MUSIC
Musik

Three Great Musicians

Johann Sebastian Bach (1685–1750) was born in Eisenach. Orphaned at the age of ten and raised by his brother, young Bach was a gifted musician who became a master of the organ, the harpsichord and the violin. He wrote hundreds of musical compositions. His music includes church music as well as compositions for specific instruments and groups of instruments. Bach's last and longest employment was as organist and choir teacher at the Church of St. Thomas in Leipzig. Today, he is considered the father of Baroque music. He married twice and was the father of twenty children. A year before his death Bach became totally blind. The *Brandenburg Concertos*, *The Well-Tempered Clavier* and the *Christmas Oratorio* are three of his many famous works.

Wolfgang Amadeus Mozart (1756–1791) was born in Salzburg, Austria. He was educated by his father, an accomplished musician, and was writing minuets at the age of five. At six, Mozart performed as a child prodigy for the royal courts of Europe.

Mozart is the finest representative of the Classical period of music. His fame resided in his ability to learn, reproduce from memory and create masterpieces effortlessly.

He wrote operas, symphonies, chamber music and church music. In spite of his superb talent and musical genius, Mozart never earned enough to support his wife and children. He died at the age of thirty-five and was buried in a pauper's grave. His masterpieces include *Eine Kleine Nachtmusik* (chamber music), *The Magic Flute* (opera) and the *Jupiter Symphony*.

Ludwig van Beethoven (1770–1827) was born in Bonn, then a small village on the Rhine River. He was introduced to music at an early age and soon became an organist at the Elector's court in Bonn. Beethoven left his home in Bonn to study in Vienna, the musical capital of Europe at the time. Although recalled to Bonn by family problems, he did return to Vienna to study under Haydn. Beethoven became interested in the democratic ideals of the French Revolution and in the Romantics' view of nature and beauty. He often reflected these interests in his music. His opera *Fidelio* and his *Fifth* and *Sixth Symphonies* are good examples of these interests.

In Vienna the composer soon became an established musician. In spite of his international fame, Beethoven had to suffer many personal tragedies. His last twelve years were spent in total deafness. Beethoven is acclaimed today as the greatest composer of the Romantic era.

 Sie spielt die erste Geige.   She plays the first fiddle.

Exercises

A Give the full name and the dates of the composer who:

1. could effortlessly memorize and play musical compositions. _____

2. composed mainly for church services and individual instruments. _____

3. started his career as an organist at the Elector's court. _____

B Verbinde B mit A.

A	**B**
1. *Jupiter Symphony* _____	a. symphony by Beethoven
2. *Brandenburg Concertos* _____	b. home of Bach
3. *Fifth Symphony* _____	c. symphony by Mozart
4. Salzburg _____	d. instrumental works by Bach
5. Leipzig _____	e. birthplace of Mozart

C Guess who...

1. was a child prodigy. _____

2. was a pupil of Haydn. _____

3. wrote pieces for the harpsichord and organ. _____

4. became deaf. _____

5. became blind. _____

D Complete the analogies.

1. Ludwig: van Beethoven = _____: Bach

2. *The Well-Tempered Clavier*: _____ = *Eine Kleine Nachtmusik*: Mozart

3. _____: Beethoven = *The Magic Flute*: Mozart

4. Bach: Eisenach = Mozart: _____

5. harpsichord music: Bach = minuets: _____

E Verbinde B mit A.

A	**B**
1. Bach _____	a. Romantic music
2. Mozart _____	b. Baroque music
3. Beethoven _____	c. Classical music

F   Verbinde den Namen mit der Abbildung!

Mozart

Bach

Beethoven

G Schreib die Namen richtig.

1. HACB _____

2. HOBNEETVE _____

3. TARZOM _____

4. SUEDAAM _____

5. NNOHJA _____

Kreuzworträtsel

H

Vertical

1. birthplace of Beethoven
2. Beethoven's kind of music
3. birthplace of Bach
4. Mozart was a child . . . .
5. birthplace of Mozart
6. Bach's *Brandenburg* . . . .

Horizontal

1. Bach's kind of music
6. Mozart's kind of music
7. Beethoven's first name
8. a Mozart symphony

JOHANN
SEBASTIAN
BACH

Bärenreiter

WEATHER AND SEASONS
Wetter und Jahreszeiten

Wie ist das Wetter?　　　How's the weather?

Es ist schön.　　　So, so.　　　Es ist schlecht.

Es ist sonnig.	It's sunny.	Es ist kühl.	It's cool.
Es ist warm.	It's warm.	Es ist windig.	It's windy.
Es ist heiß.	It's hot.	Es ist schwül.	It's humid.
		Es ist wolkig.	It's cloudy.

Es ist kalt.	It's cold.
Es blitzt.	It's lightning.
Es schneit.	It's snowing.
Es donnert.	It's thundering.
Es regnet.	It's raining.

Welche Jahreszeit haben wir?　　　What's the season?
Wir haben . . .　　　It's . . .

Die vier Jahreszeiten

der Frühling

der Herbst

der Winter

der Sommer

 Use "im" before a season:
"im Sommer" = in the summer

 Der April macht die Blumen,　　April showers
und der Mai hat den Dank dafür.　　bring May flowers.

A Verbinde den Satz mit der Abbildung!

1. _____ a. Es ist sonnig.

2. _____ b. Es blitzt.

3. _____ c. Es regnet.

4. _____ d. Es ist windig.

5. _____ e. Es ist kalt.

B Wie ist das Wetter? Beantworte die Frage auf Deutsch!

1. _____

2. _____

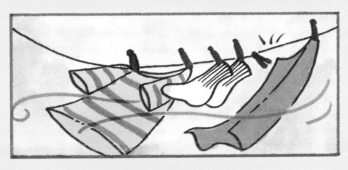

3. _____

4. _____

5. _____

c Verbinde die Jahreszeit mit der Abbildung!

1. _____ a. Sommer

2. _____ b. Winter

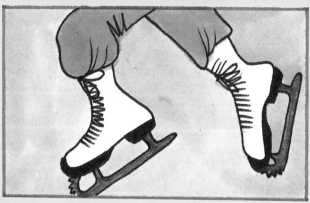

3. _____ c. Frühling

4. _____ d. Herbst

D Write in column one the English for each word at the left. When you have finished the entire column, cover the column of words at the left, and in column two, write the English words in German.

	column one	**column two**
	(English)	*(German)*
1. Sonne	1._____	1._____
2. Blitz	2._____	2._____
3. Frühling	3._____	3._____
4. Sommer	4._____	4._____
5. Wetter	5._____	5._____
6. Herbst	6._____	6._____
7. Jahreszeit	7._____	7._____
8. kühl	8._____	8._____
9. heiß	9._____	9._____
10. Es regnet.	10._____	10._____
11. Winter	11._____	11._____
12. schlecht	12._____	12._____
13. Donner	13._____	13._____
14. kalt	14._____	14._____

E Verbinde B mit A.

A	**B**
nouns	*verbs*
1. Regen _____	a. donnern
2. Schnee _____	b. schneien
3. Donner _____	c. regnen
4. Blitz _____	d. scheinen
5. Sonne _____	e. blitzen

F Wie ist das Wetter? (Auf Deutsch, bitte.) *Using the cue at the left, write a statement about the weather.*

1. mittens and parka _____

2. sunglasses _____

3. lightning bolts _____

4. cardigan sweater _____

5. outdoor tennis court _____

6. umbrella _____

7. snowflakes _____

8. air conditioner _____

9. sailboat _____

10. rain, wind and hail _____

G Lies den Absatz und dann wähle die richtigen Antworten!

Die vier Jahreszeiten

Im Winter ist es sehr kalt und es schneit oft. Der Schnee ist weiß. Im Frühling ist es windig, kühl und regnerisch. Das Wetter im Sommer ist sonnig und heiß. Im Herbst ist es wieder kühl und windig. Die vier Jahreszeiten sind wunderbar.

1. Wie viele Jahreszeiten gibt es?
   a. eine
   b. vier
   c. zwei
   d. drei

2. Wie ist das Wetter im Winter?
   a. Es ist Winter.
   b. Es ist schön.
   c. Es ist warm.
   d. Es ist kalt.

3. Im Frühling ist es....
   a. regnerisch
   b. heiß
   c. kalt
   d. weiß

4. Die Sonne scheint viel im....
   a. Sommer
   b. Herbst
   c. Frühling
   d. Winter

Kreuzworträtsel

H

Vertical

2. When water runs off a duck's back, "es..."
3. When dazzling streaks illuminate the sky, "es..."
5. season of floral rebirth
6. harvest season (temperate zone)
7. skiing season
9. hazy, hot and muggy
11. not very "kalt"
13. "Es regnet...Herbst."

Horizontal

1. Dinner rolls should be served...
4. A hazy day is...
7. what everyone talks about
8. Winter is a...(of four seasons)
9. very nice out
10. time for picnics and swimming
11. Ice cubes are...
12. March is traditionally...
14. normal summer temperature (ß = ss)

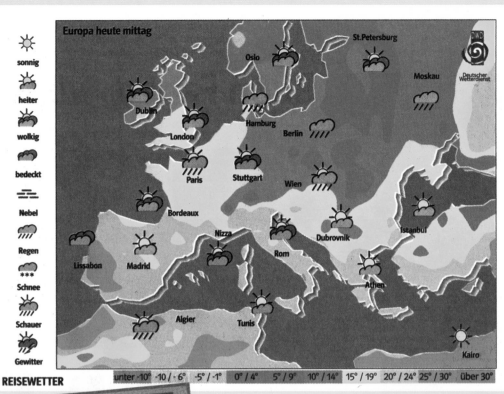

Europa heute mittag

sonnig
heiter
wolkig
bedeckt
Nebel
Regen
Schnee
Schauer
Gewitter

REISEWETTER

St.Petersburg • Moskau • Oslo • Dublin • Hamburg • London • Berlin • Paris • Stuttgart • Wien • Istanbul • Bordeaux • Nizza • Dubrovnik • Rom • Lissabon • Madrid • Athen • Algier • Tunis • Kairo

| unter -10° | -10 / -6° | -5° / -1° | 0° / 4° | 5° / 9° | 10° / 14° | 15° / 19° | 20° / 24° | 25° / 30° | über 30° |

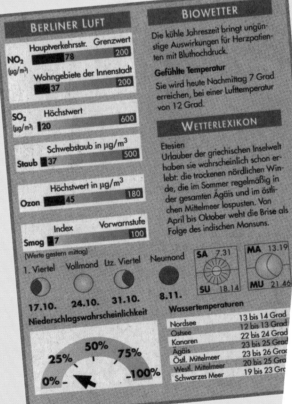

BERLINER LUFT

	Hauptverkehrsstr.	Grenzwert
NO₂ [µg/m³]	78	200

Wohngebiete der Innenstadt
37 — 200

	Höchstwert	
SO₂ [µg/m³]	20	600

Schwebstaub in µg/m³
Staub 37 — 500

Höchstwert in µg/m³
Ozon 45 — 180

Index Vorwarnstufe
Smog 7 — 100

(Werte gestern mittag)

1. Viertel	Vollmond	Ltz. Viertel	Neumond		SA 7.31	MA 13.19
					SU 18.14	MU 21.46
17.10.	24.10.	31.10.	8.11.			

Niederschlagswahrscheinlichkeit

25% 50% 75%
0% - -100%

BIOWETTER

Die kühle Jahreszeit bringt ungünstige Auswirkungen für Herzpatienten mit Bluthochdruck.

Gefühlte Temperatur

Sie wird heute Nachmittag 7 Grad erreichen, bei einer Lufttemperatur von 12 Grad.

WETTERLEXIKON

Etesien
Urlauber der griechischen Inselwelt haben sie wahrscheinlich schon erlebt: die trockenen nördlichen Winde, die im Sommer regelmäßig in der gesamten Ägäis und im östlichen Mittelmeer lospusten. Von April bis Oktober weht die Brise als Folge des indischen Monsuns.

Wassertemperaturen

Nordsee	13 bis 14 Grad
Ostsee	12 bis 13 Grad
Kanaren	22 bis 24 Grad
Ägäis	23 bis 25 Grad
Östl. Mittelmeer	23 bis 26 Grad
Westl. Mittelmeer	20 bis 25 Grad
Schwarzes Meer	19 bis 23 Grad

DAS WETTER

Nach Nebel wechselnd bewölkt

Warmfront
Kaltfront
Mischfront
T Tief H Hoch

Faröer 8° • Stockholm 11° • Helsinki 12° • London 13° • H • Düsseldorf 14° • Warschau 12° • Paris 13° • Wien 13° • Madrid 21° • Rom 22° • Lissabon 23° • Istanbul 24° • Las Palmas 26° • Tunis 24° • Athen 27°

Temperaturen in Europa, gestern 13 Uhr

Amsterdam	12°	Istanbul	24°	Paris	13°	Tunis	22°
Athen	29°	Lissabon	23°	Prag	20°	Warschau	11°
Barcelona	18°	Madrid	20°	Rom	20°	Wien	13°
Berlin	11°	Moskau	24°	Stockholm	13°	Zürich	12°

104

16

DAYS AND MONTHS
Tage und Monate

Welcher Tag ist heute?
Heute ist...

What day is today?
Today is...

Monday Montag	Dienstag	Mittwoch	Donnerstag	Freitag	Samstag (Sonnabend)	Sonntag
	1	2	3	4	5	6
7	8	9	10	11	12	13
14	15	16	17	18	19	20
21	22	23	24	25	26	27
28	29	30	31			

Welches Datum haben wir?
Heute ist der erste Mai.

What is the date today?
It's May first today.

April
Mai
Juni

Oktober
November
Dezember

Januar
Februar
März

Juli
August
September

Morgen, morgen, nur nicht
heute, sagen alle faulen Leute.

Don't put off until tomorrow
what you can do today.

Weekdays and Mythology
Derivations and Comparisons

German Day	Norse Mythology
Montag	day honoring the moon god "Mond" = moon
Dienstag	day honoring Tyr, a Norse god of war, and/or Mars Thingsus, the Roman god of war The latter was also known as God of the Assembly and Protector of the Tribal Councils. "Dienstag" was Tribal Council Day.
Mittwoch	day honoring Wodan or Odin, father of the gods and a god of war Wodan's Day = Wednesday Wodan often wore a hat with a wide brim and carried a large staff. The Romans compared him to Mercury with his caduseus or staff.
Donnerstag	day honoring Thor, god of weather and thunder, and son of Wodan Thor = Donner = thunder Thor's Day = Thursday Thor always carried an enormous hammer. The Romans found him similar to Hercules and his club.
Freitag	day honoring Freia, goddess of love, and wife of Wodan. The Romans compared her to their goddess Venus.
Samstag	day honoring Saturn, Roman god of the harvest and agriculture
Sonntag	day honoring the sun god "Sonne" = sun

Jakobs Heft
Lerne für die Englischarbeit!

1. tomorrow (mein Geburtstag)
2. the day after tomorrow
3. yesterday
4. the day before yesterday
5. the day
6. the holiday (Bravo!)
7. the school day (Mensch!)
8. the birthday (morgen)
9. the week
10. the weekend (mein Leben)
11. the month

Jakob's Notebook
Learn for English test:

1. morgen
2. übermorgen
3. gestern
4. vorgestern
5. der Tag
6. der Feiertag
7. der Schultag
8. der Geburtstag
9. die Woche
10. das Wochenende
11. der Monat

Exercises

A Write in numerical form the dates which your teacher reads.

1. _____

2. _____

3. _____

4. _____

5. _____

B Label the current month. Include the names of the days and all the numbers.

MONAT _____

TAG	TAG	TAG	TAG	TAG	TAG	TAG

C Schreib die Daten!

1. Wednesday, December 25th _____

2. Saturday, November 11th _____

3. Thursday, May 1st _____

4. Sunday, June 17th _____

5. Monday, April 19th _____

D Complete the following in English.

1. If the date is 9.1.2003 (German date), what is the month?

   _____

2. What happens when Thor, the weathergod, strikes his hammer? Explain what you hear.

   _____

3. Identify the family of gods represented in the weekdays.

   mother _____

   father _____

   son _____

E Verbinde B mit A.

A	B
1. übermorgen _____	a. tomorrow
2. heute _____	b. yesterday
3. morgen _____	c. day before yesterday
4. vorgestern _____	d. day after tomorrow
5. gestern _____	e. today

F Schreib auf Deutsch!

1. the day after "Mittwoch" _____

2. the two summer vacation months _____

3. the day that was "vorgestern" _____

4. the "Monat" that begins the calendar year _____

5. the day that is "morgen" _____

6. your favorite day _____

7. your garbage collection day _____

8. your "Geburtstag" month _____

G Schreib den deutschen Tag der Abbildung nach!

1. _____

2. _____

3. _____

4. _____

5. _____

6. _____

7. _____

H Lies den Absatz! Wähle die richtigen Antworten!

Heute ist Freitag und das ist fantastisch. Das Wochenende kommt. Am Samstag ist ein Fußballspiel. Die deutsche Mannschaft spielt gegen Frankreich. Meine Freunde und ich interessieren uns sehr für Fußball. Wir spielen sehr oft Fußball. Sonntag ist Familientag. Ich gehe am Sonntag mit meiner Familie spazieren. Wir sprechen oft über Fußball, das Wetter, die Schule und die kommende Woche. Das Wochenende ist bald da!

der Fußball	soccer
das Spiel	game
die Mannschaft	team
spielen	to play
gegen	against
spazieren	(to go) walking
sprechen	to speak
bald	soon

1. Warum ist Freitag fantastisch?
   a. Das Wetter ist schön.
   b. Heute ist Freitag.
   c. Ich spreche über Fußball.
   d. Das Wochenende kommt.

2. Wann ist das Fußballspiel?
   a. am Freitag
   b. am Samstag
   c. am Sonntag
   d. am Montag

3. Ist Fußball mein Hobby?
   a. ja
   b. nein

4. Was mache ich am Sonntag?
   a. Ich gehe spazieren.
   b. Ich spiele Fußball.
   c. Ich gehe in die Schule.
   d. Ich interessiere mich für Fußball.

5. Wer geht mit mir spazieren?
   a. mein Fußball
   b. mein Fisch
   c. meine Familie
   d. meine Freunde

Kreuzworträtsel

Vertical

1. birthmonth of Washington and Lincoln
2. day honoring the goddess of love
4. month of American independence
5. One attends classes on a...
6. from Friday afternoon until Sunday evening
7. noisy day of the week
9. opposite of "Abend"
10. moonday
11. date
14. "dog days" month

Horizontal

3. "gestern,...und morgen"
4. month of the year's first holiday
8. month in which summer begins
9. day in the middle of the week
10. month of Martians
12. Today is the tomorrow worried about...
13. day honoring the god of heat and light
15. "Guten...."
16. a weekend day
17. the most necessary day in a person's life

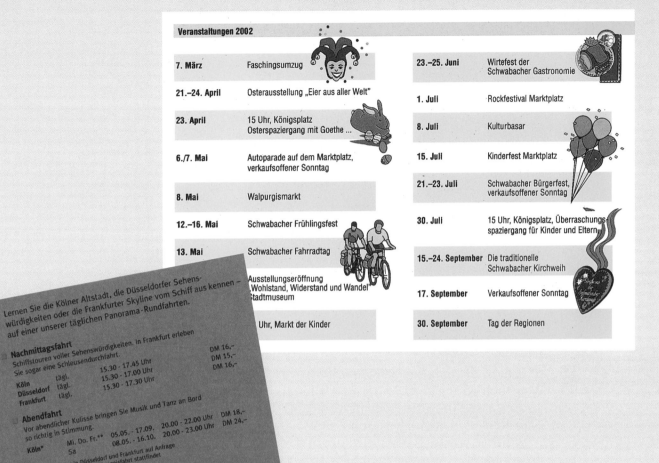

Veranstaltungen 2002

7. März	Faschingsumzug
21.–24. April	Osterausstellung „Eier aus aller Welt"
23. April	15 Uhr, Königsplatz Osterspaziergang mit Goethe ...
6./7. Mai	Autoparade auf dem Marktplatz, verkaufsoffener Sonntag
8. Mai	Walpurgismarkt
12.–16. Mai	Schwabacher Frühlingsfest
13. Mai	Schwabacher Fahrradtag
	Ausstellungseröffnung „Wohlstand, Widerstand und Wandel" Stadtmuseum
	Uhr, Markt der Kinder
23.–25. Juni	Wirtefest der Schwabacher Gastronomie
1. Juli	Rockfestival Marktplatz
8. Juli	Kulturbasar
15. Juli	Kinderfest Marktplatz
21.–23. Juli	Schwabacher Bürgerfest, verkaufsoffener Sonntag
30. Juli	15 Uhr, Königsplatz, Überraschungsspaziergang für Kinder und Eltern
15.–24. September	Die traditionelle Schwabacher Kirchweih
17. September	Verkaufsoffener Sonntag
30. September	Tag der Regionen

Lernen Sie die Kölner Altstadt, die Düsseldorfer Sehenswürdigkeiten oder die Frankfurter Skyline vom Schiff aus kennen – auf einer unserer täglichen Panorama-Rundfahrten.

Nachmittagsfahrt
Schiffstouren voller Sehenswürdigkeiten. In Frankfurt erleben Sie sogar eine Schleusendurchfahrt.

Köln	tägl.	15.30 - 17.45 Uhr	DM 16,–
Düsseldorf	tägl.	15.30 - 17.00 Uhr	DM 15,–
Frankfurt	tägl.	15.30 - 17.30 Uhr	DM 16,–

Abendfahrt
Vor abendlicher Kulisse bringen Sie Musik und Tanz an Bord so richtig in Stimmung.

Köln*	Mi. Do. Fr.**	05.05. - 17.09.	20.00 - 22.00 Uhr	DM 18,–
	Sa	08.05. - 16.10.	20.00 - 23.00 Uhr	DM 24,–

* Abendfahrten in Düsseldorf und Frankfurt auf Anfrage
** nur wenn freitags keine Ereignisfahrt stattfindet

Tagesfahrt nach Zons
Schiffsausflug und Stadtbesichtigung in einer Tour.
Von Düsseldorf nach Zons und zurück.

Düsseldorf	Mo.	14. u. 28.06.	10.00 - 19.00 Uhr	DM 29,–
	Mo.	12. u. 26.07.		
	Mo.	09. u. 23.08.		
	Mo.	06. u. 20.09.		

(Ausstieg in Zons möglich, Ankunft 12.00 Uhr, nur Hinfahrt DM 19,–)

Kaffeefahrt nach Zons
Ein gemütlicher Tag auf dem Rhein. Mit Kaffee, Klatsch und guter Laune.

Köln	Mi.	07. u. 21.07.	11.30 - 19.00 Uhr	DM 29,–
	Mi.	04. u. 18.08.		
	Mi.	01. u. 15.09.		

(Ausstieg in Zons möglich, Ankunft 13.30 Uhr, nur Hinfahrt DM 25,–)

Tagesfahrt nach Köln
Mit dieser Schiffstour von Düsseldorf aus ein ganz besonderes Vergnügen.

Düsseldorf	Mo.	14. u. 28.06.	10.00 - 19.00 Uhr	DM 36,–
	Mo.	12. u. 26.07.		
	Mo.	09. u. 23.08.		
	Mo.	06. u. 20.09.		

Brunch-Fahrt
Genießen, genießen und nochmal genießen: das Brunch-Buffet, die gute Musik, tolle Atmosphäre – eine Schiffstour zum Schlemmen.

Köln 1. u. 3. So. im Monat Mai bis Oktober 10.30 - 13.15 Uhr
Erwachsene DM 39,– Kinder DM 15,–

Terminvorschau

Schulferien in Niedersachsen:

Jahr	Ostern	Pfingsten	Sommer	Herbst	Weihnachten
1999	29.03.–17.04.	25.05.	22.07–01.09.	18.10.–01.11.	23.12.1999–08.01.2000
2000	14.04.–29.04.	13.06.	13.07.–23.08.	19.10.–01.11.	22.12.2000–06.01.2001
2001	30.03.–17.04.	05.06.	28.06.–08.08.	01.10.–13.10.	24.12.2001–05.01.2002
2002	25.03.–13.04.	21.05.	20.06.–31.07.	30.09.–12.10.	23.12.2002–06.01.2003

Five Great Authors

Johann Wolfgang von Goethe (1749–1832), considered by many to be Germany's greatest writer, was born in Frankfurt. He received an excellent education at several universities. Goethe excelled in law, art, science, politics and literature. His studies allowed him to hold many outstanding positions. He was a statesman, a theater director, a newspaper editor and an internationally famous poet, dramatist and novelist. Goethe's work enabled him to travel widely and his command of languages permitted him to be at home almost anywhere. In his famous Classical drama, *Faust*, Goethe places desire for temporal fame and knowledge in conflict with spiritual values. This famous work inspired both Gounod and Berlioz to write operas presenting this conflict.

Friedrich Schiller (1759–1805) was born in the little city of Marbach on the Neckar River. Although he studied law and medicine, he preferred literature. He became a writer at the Mannheim Theater, a professor of history at Jena, and a friend of Goethe at Weimar.

Schiller wrote many plays dealing with classical ideals, especially freedom. His characters deal with human problems and must make important decisions. In *Maria Stuart* the Scottish Queen, Mary Stuart, accepts her unjust imprisonment by Elisabeth as atonement for her own misdeeds. In the patriotic play, *Wilhelm Tell*, the hero chooses between the possible death of his son and the freedom of the Swiss people. In the poem *An die Freude* ("Ode to Joy"), Schiller shares his belief that love can make the world a better place. Beethoven incorporated this poem into his *Ninth Symphony*.

Ernst Theodor Amadeus Hoffmann (1776–1822) was born in Königsberg on the Baltic Sea. Out of love for Mozart he changed his second middle name from Wilhelm to Amadeus. He was also an ardent fan of Beethoven. Too much work and lack of enough attention to his health led to his early death.

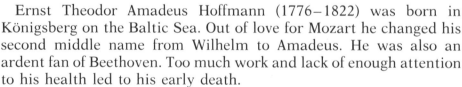

E.T.A. Hoffmann's writing has influenced authors in other nations, especially Charles Baudelaire in France and Edgar Allan Poe in the United States. A collection of his stories called *Nachtstücke* inspired Offenbach's opera, *Les Contes d' Hoffmann*. *Nussknacker und Mäusekönig* inspired Tchaikowsky's musical work, *The Nutcracker Suite*. The stories of Hoffmann are Romantic. They deal with imagination, and the many opposites in everyday life; joy and sorrow, good and evil, and dreams and reality.

 Ende gut, alles gut.   All's well, that ends well.

The poet, playwright, and essayist Else Lasker-Schüler (1869-1945) was born in Elberfeld, a small village near Wuppertal. She was raised in a warm and loving home and was devastated when her parents and brother died. Eventually she found some consolation in literature and art. Historical practices and traditions had made it difficult for most women to be well educated, but changes in the late nineteenth and early twentieth centuries provided increased opportunities for women authors. Lasker-Schüler took advantage of the opportunities and joined the exciting circle of Berlin's Expressionists. She contributed to new literary magazines and wrote several volumes of poetry and prose that she decorated with her own lithographs and drawings. Her works were praised by such distinguished celebrities as poet Gottfried Benn and Franz Marc, an artist in the famous "Blue Rider" community.

Later years brought the poet a renewed sense of loss, as her second marriage failed and her son died. When the literary and political climate of Berlin changed, Lasker-Schüler emigrated to Palestine and lived in Jerusalem until her death.

Most of Lasker-Schüler's poems, in volumes entitled *Styx*, *Der siebente Tag*, and *Hebräische Balladen*, focus on the themes of love, friendship, and loss. They show the poet's unusual use of language, contain colorful imagery and references to mythology, and, in general, reflect the free spirit of the Expressionist movement. Lasker-Schüler is a respected leader in early twentieth century literature. Gottfried Benn called her the greatest woman lyric poet of Germany.

Christa Wolf is a contemporary novelist and literary critic. She was born in 1929 in Landsberg, a small town once in Germany but now in Poland. Her parents owned a small store and Wolf enjoyed a quiet middle-class upbringing. World War II, however, and its aftermath brought harsh realities and severe hardships. Her family had to join the thousands of refugees who were forced to leave their homes and march westward.

After secondary school in 1949, Wolf began to identify with the political and social ideals of the new German Democratic Republic. University studies and discussions with the well-established author Anna Seghers helped the young woman decide on a literary career.

Wolf's first novel, *Der geteilte Himmel*, received tremendous worldwide attention and soon appeared as a motion picture. It concerns two young people whose lives and love are disrupted by the politics of East versus West. A second novel, *Nachdenken über Christa W.*, and other stories show how societies and governments can interfere with an individual's personal liberty and self-esteem.

Exercises

A Guess who...

1. loved the music of Mozart and Beethoven. _____

2. was a statesman and scientist as well as an author. _____

3. was an artist as well as a writer. _____

4. studied medicine. _____

5. wrote about politics and love. _____

B Verbinde B mit A.

A	B
1. Else Lasker-Schüler _____	a. Schiller
2. "Romantic" stories _____	b. are about ideals.
3. Friedrich _____	c. Expressionist poet
4. "Classical" stories _____	d. Hoffmann
5. Ernst Theodor Amadeus _____	e. are about dreams and imagination.

C Using the example, complete the chart below.

Name of work	Author	Type of Musical Rendition	Composer(s)
example			
Wilhelm Tell (William Tell)	Schiller	opera	Rossini
1. *Nachtstücke* (Night-Pieces)	_____	_____	_____
2. *An die Freude* (Ode to Joy)	_____	_____	_____
3. *Nussknacker und Mäusekönig* (Nutcracker and Mouse-King)	_____	_____	_____
4. *Faust*	_____	_____	_____
			_____

D Complete the analogies.

1. plays and poetry: Schiller = _____: Hoffmann

2. Goethe: _____ = Schiller: *Maria Stuart*

3. Königsberg: Hoffmann = _____: Schiller

4. _____: knowledge = *Wilhelm Tell*: freedom

5. "Ode to Joy": _____ = *Nutcracker and Mouse-King*: story

6. _____: C. Wolf = poems: Lasker-Schüler

E Which author would most likely...

1. encourage a child to get a well-rounded education?_____

2. enjoy creating new words and puns? _____

3. explain historical events in Europe? _____

4. write a script for a horror or science-fiction film? _____

5. help a child develop personal goals and self-esteem?_____

6. wear an "I Love Mozart and Beethoven" T-shirt? _____

F Label each plot described below as either Classical or Romantic.

1. Eunice Unity is working this summer at Camp Ideal. Her job is to organize the children into activity groups and to direct a variety show for the benefit of underprivileged children. On this particular day the campers are squabbling about who has the most talent and who will perform first. Eunice arrives on the scene, and in a short time transforms the children from selfish creatures into helpful and compassionate young people.

   _____

2. While riding your horse one late moonlit evening, you come to a fork in the road. A sign pointing to the left says: "This way to that way." A sign pointing to the right says: "That way to this way." Just as you are about to make your decision, a cloud passes in front of the moon, an owl shrieks and a bat flies into your face.

   _____

Hoffmann

Goethe

Schiller

H Ergänze die Sätze!

1. _____ taught history at the university in Jena.

2. _____ had a great influence on literature in France and the United States.

3. _____ was a friend of Anna Seghers.

4. _____ was exceptionally good in everything he studied.

5. _____ was interested in the choices and decisions people had to make.

6. _____ wrote unusual lyric poetry.

7. _____ was put into jail by Queen Elisabeth.

8. _____ was a national hero in Switzerland.

9. _____ und _____ inspired Tchaikowsky.

10. _____ made a deal with the devil in exchange for knowledge.

HERZLICHE GRÜSSE AUS
FRANKFURT AM MAIN

Lieber Engel, ich bin ganz Dein

Goethes schönste Briefe an Frauen. Hg. Angelika Maass
Mit zahlr. Abb.
it 2150. 390 Seiten
DM 19,80/öS 145,-/sFr. 19.-

Goethe war sein Leben lang in seinem Element, wenn er Verwandten, Freundinnen, Geliebten schreiben, wenn er ihnen Geständnisse machen, von Reisen oder den Dingen seines Alltags berichten konnte.
Ausgewählt wurden Briefe an Frauen, die von besonderer Bedeutung für ihn waren.

■ Goethes Morgenland-fahrten

West-östliche Begegnungen
Hg. Jochen Golz
Originalausgabe
it 2600. 320 Seiten
DM 29,80/öS 218,-/sFr. 27.50

Lebenslang war Goethe von der Kultur des Orients fasziniert nicht zuletzt der *West-östliche Divan* gibt Zeugnis davon. Das Goethe- und Schiller-Archiv in Weimar zeigt ab 26. Mai in einer großen Ausstellung *Goethes Morgenlandfahrten* Exponate einer hochstehenden Schriftkultur und gibt Einblick in Goethes Dichterwerkstatt.

■ Goethe Die Kunst des Lebens

Aus seinen Werken, Briefen und Gesprächen
Hg. Katharina Mommsen
Mitwirkung: Elke Richter
Originalausgabe
it 2525. 180 Seiten
DM 14,80/öS 108,-/sFr. 14.-

Goethes realistische Überlebensstrategien sind reich an Weltkenntnis, Witz und echter Weisheit. Als Lebenskünstler, der er selber geworden war, hinterließ er der Welt in seinen Werken, Briefen und Gesprächen eine riesige Apotheke voller Heilmittel und Rezepte, die auch heute noch ihre Wirkung tun können.

Goethe Sein Leben in Bildern und Texten

Vorwort: Adolf Muschg
Hg. Christoph Michel
Gestaltung: Willy Fleckhaus
it 1000. 413 Seiten
DM 24,-/öS 175,-/sFr. 22.-

Keine Nachinszenierung von Goethes Leben, sondern ein Buch, das der kombinatorischen Phantasie des Lesers Spielraum läßt. Es entsteht der Eindruck eines nach allen Seiten ausgreifenden, immer neu ansetzenden Experiments, von Goethe in einer Vornotiz für *Dichtung und Wahrheit* auf die Formel gebracht: „Mein Leben ein einziges Abenteuer."

MUSEEN

Armeemuseum (im Neuen Schloss): Geöffnet Di bis So 8.45 bis 16.30 Uhr. Abteilung Erster Weltkrieg (im Reduit Tilly): Öffnungszeiten wie oben. Jeden 1. So im Monat um 14 Uhr Führung im Neuen Schloss.
Medizinhistorisches Museum, Anatomiestr. 18–20: Geöffnet Di bis So 10 bis 12 Uhr und 14 bis 17 Uhr, Mo geschlossen.
Stadtmuseum Ingolstadt (Kavalier Hepp), Auf der Schanz 45: Geöffnet Di bis Sa 9 bis 17 Uhr, So 10 bis 17 Uhr, Mo geschlossen. Jeden 2. und 4. So im Monat um 14 Uhr Führungen.
Spielzeugmuseum im Stadtmuseum: Öffnungszeiten wie Stadtmuseum. Jeden 1. So im Monat von 13.30 bis 16.30 Uhr Vorführung O-Spur-Tinplate-Anlage, jeden 3. So 13.30 bis 16.30 Uhr Vorführung Märklin 00 (HO).
Museum für Konkrete Kunst, Tränktorstr. 6–8: Geöffnet Di u. Do bis So 10 bis 18 Uhr, Mi 10 bis 14 Uhr u. 17 bis 21 Uhr.
Bauerngerätemuseum Hundszell: Geöffnet Di bis Fr 9 bis 12 Uhr, So 14 bis 17 Uhr.

Johann Wolfgang von Goethe

18

LEISURE AND RECREATION
Freizeit

Wohin gehst du? Where are you going?

Ich gehe zum Fußballspiel.
I'm going to the soccer game.

Ich gehe ins Museum.
I'm going to the museum.

Ich gehe auf die Party.
I'm going to the party.

Ich gehe zum Strand.
I'm going to the beach.

Andreas:	Wohin gehst du heute Abend?		Where are you going tonight?
Heiko:	Ich gehe zum Fußballspiel.		I'm going to the soccer game.
Andreas:	Ich auch.		Me, too.

❀❀❀❀❀❀

Peter:	Was machst du heute?		What are you doing today?
Tina:	Ich gehe ins Museum...in die Alte Pinakothek*.		I'm going to the museum...to the *Alte Pinakothek*.
Peter:	Was ist da los?		What's going on there?
Tina:	Das Dürerfest findet diese Woche statt.		The Dürer Festival is taking place this week.

* The Alte Pinakothek, *an art museum in* München, *houses paintings and artworks from the 14th to the 18th centuries. Its counterpart, the* Neue Pinakothek, *contains art generally from the 19th and 20th centuries.*

In der Abwechslung liegt das Vergnügen. Variety is the spice of life.

Ich spiele Volleyball.
I play volleyball.

Ich spiele Fußball.
I play soccer.

Welche Sportart treibst du?
What sports do you play?

Ich spiele Basketball.
I play basketball.

Ich spiele Tennis.
I play tennis.

Ich spiele Baseball.
I play baseball.

Was machst du gern?
What do you like to do?

Ich laufe gern Ski.
I like skiing.

Ich reite gern.
I like horseback riding.

Ich lese gern.
I like reading.

Ich tanze gern.
I like dancing.

Ich schwimme gern.
I like swimming.

Ich fahre gern Rad.
I like biking.

Käthe:	Morgen machen wir ein Picknick.	Tomorrow we'll have a picnic.
Julia:	Wo denn?	Where's that?
Käthe:	Am Strand. Willst du mitkommen?	At the beach. Do you want to come along?
Julia:	Ja. Ich schwimme gern.	Yes. I like swimming.

❋❋❋❋❋

Jutta:	Gehst du heute Abend auf die Party?	Are you going to the party tonight?
Thomas:	Na klar. Gibt es da Musik?	Of course. Will there be music?
Jutta:	Ja. Ich tanze gern.	Yes. I like dancing.

A Wohin gehst du? Ergänze die Sätze auf Deutsch!

1. Ich gehe zu einem _____ . (*soccer game*)

2. Ich gehe zu einem _____ . (*picnic*)

3. Ich gehe auf eine _____ . (*party*)

4. Ich gehe in ein _____ . (*museum*)

5. Ich gehe zum _____ . (*beach*)

B Select the correct answers based on the previous dialogues.

1. Wann ist das Fußballspiel?
   - a. am Montag
   - b. um vier Uhr
   - c. heute Abend
   - d. in zwei Wochen

2. Was ist die Alte Pinakothek?
   - a. ein Strand
   - b. ein Rad
   - c. ein Dürerfest
   - d. ein Museum

3. Wer ist Dürer?
   - a. ein Lehrer
   - b. ein Onkel
   - c. ein Museum
   - d. ein Künstler

4. Wann ist das Picknick?
   - a. morgen
   - b. heute
   - c. am Sonntag
   - d. um ein Uhr

5. Wo ist das Picknick?
   - a. am Mittwoch
   - b. am Dienstag
   - c. am Strand
   - d. am Museum

C Welche Sportart treibst du? Ergänze die Sätze auf Deutsch!

1. Ich spiele _____.

2. Ich spiele _____.

3. Ich spiele _____.

4. Ich spiele _____.

5. Ich spiele _____.

D Schreib die Wörter richtig.

1. FRTZEEII

2. NSDATR

3. KSUIM

4. WIMMSCHEN

5. REENTI

E Was machst du gern? Ergänze die Sätze auf Deutsch!

1. Ich _____ gern Ski.

2. Ich _____ gern.

3. Ich _____ gern ein Buch.

4. Ich _____ gern Rad.

5. Ich _____ gern.

6. Ich _____ gern.

F Ergänze den Dialog auf Deutsch.

Timo: Was machst _____ am Freitag abend?

Ali: _____ gehe zu Christines Haus.

Timo: Was ist da _____ ?

Ali: Eine Party _____ da statt.

Timo: Wie viele kommen zur _____ ?

Ali: Neun. Fünf _____ und vier Jungen.

Timo: Gut. Ich _____ auch. Gibt es da auch

_____ ?

Ali: Na klar. Ich tanze _____ .

G Lies den Absatz! Wähle die richtigen Antworten!

Martina plant eine Geburtstagsparty am Strand. Heute ist sie zwölf Jahre alt. Am Samstag wird sie dreizehn. Wer kommt zur Party? Ihre Freunde: Anja, Luise, Patrick, Boris und Dieter. Die Party ist um drei Uhr. Ihre Freunde sind froh. Sie spielen gern Volleyball. Sie schwimmen, tanzen und machen auch ein Picknick. Eine Geburtstagsparty am Strand ist eine prima Idee!

die Geburtstagsparty	birthday party
wird	(she will) turn, become
Freunde	friends
froh	happy
prima	terrific

1. Wie alt ist Martina heute?
   - a. dreizehn
   - b. zwölf
   - c. drei
   - d. elf

2. Wie viele Jungen kommen zur Party?
   - a. drei
   - b. zwölf
   - c. dreizehn
   - d. zwei

3. Wann ist Martinas Geburtstag?
   - a. am Sonntag
   - b. am Montag
   - c. am Donnerstag
   - d. am Samstag

4. Wo essen die Mädchen und Jungen gern?
   - a. in einem Restaurant
   - b. am Strand
   - c. in der Küche
   - d. im Esszimmer

5. Was machen die Jungen und Mädchen gern?
   - a. Sie schreiben gern.
   - b. Sie schwimmen gern.
   - c. Sie wiederholen gern.
   - d. Sie lesen gern.

was wann wo

Nr. 234 / Donnerstag, 10. Oktober 2002

RADIO IN

6.00–10.00 Perfekt geweckt mit Klaus Teuber und Moni Littel 10.00–12.00 Büro und so mit Melanie Arzenheimer 12.00–13.00 Musik nonstop 13.00–15.00 Der Mittag mit Melanie Arzenheimer 15.00–18.30 Der Nachmittag mit Italo Mele 18.30–19.00 Kulturkanal 19.00–6.00 Musik nonstop Die Radio-IN-Internet-Adresse: www.radio-in.de

BUNDESLIGA

Rostock — Frankfurt 3:1 (1:0)

Rostock: Bräutigam - Benken, Holetschek, Ehlers - Weilandt (70. Radwan) - Lange, Wibran, Brand, Emara - Baumgart (85. Kovacec), Arvidsson (76. Ahanfouf).

Frankfurt: Nikolov - Kutschera (46. Dombi), Janßen, Kracht - Bindewald, Weber, Bulut, Gebhardt (67. Fjörtoft) - Guie-Mien - Yang, Salou.

Schiedsrichter: Stark (Landshut).

Tore: 1:0 Brand (35.), 2:0 Holetschek (66.), 2:1 Fjörtoft (77.), 3:1 Lange (86., Foulelfmeter).

Zuschauer: 15 000.

Gelbe Karten: Baumgart, Arvidsson, Ahanfouf - Bulut, Kracht (2), Guie-Mien.

Unterhaching — Wolfsburg 1:1 (0:0)

Unterhaching: Wittmann - Bergen - Seifert, Grassow - Haber, Matthias Zimmermann (83. Garcia), Schwarz, Kögl (79. Bucher), Straube - Oberleitner (70. Rraklli), Seitz.

Wolfsburg: Reitmaier - O'Neil, Thomsen, Biliskov - Greiner, Maltritz (67. Sebescen), Munteanu (60. Wück), Nowak, Weiser - Juskowiak (80. Feldhoff), Akpoborie.

Schiedsrichter: Berg (Konz).

Tore: 1:0 Straube (50.), 1:1 Akpoborie (71.).

Zuschauer: 8 600.

Gelbe Karten: Schwarz (3), Bergen (2) - Greiner (3), O'Neil (2).

DIE FLOTTE

Eine Klasse für sich

Groß oder klein, nostalgischer Schaufelraddampfer oder elegantes Großraumschiff, schnittiges Tragflügelboot oder gemütliches Partyschiff – mit 16 Schiffen auf Rhein, Main und Mosel ist die stolze KD-Flotte für alles zu haben: Ausflüge, Charter, viel Spaß und gute Laune!

DIE NOSTALGISCHEN

Im Goethe-Jahr fährt die GOETHE ganz auf Goethes Linie: täglich ab 9 Uhr von Koblenz nach Rüdesheim und zurück. An Bord sorgen Goethe-Menü und Goethe-Wein für kultivierten Genuß. (Anlegestellen siehe Fahrplan!)

NEU! Die KD Nostalgie-Route auf S. 8

Dampfer KRIPPEN

Dampfer GOETHE

DIE EDLEN
Modern und schnittig.

MS STOLZENFELS

MS WARSTEINER

MS JAN VON WERTH

KD 3

Panorama-Park 2002

800.000 qm
Spaß & Action in einzigartiger Natur!

PANORAMA PARK
DER GROSSE ERLEBNIS PARK
Sauerland

Kirchhundem/Kreis Olpe

19

SHOPPING
Einkaufen

der Verkäufer
salesclerk

die Kundin
customer

die Tennisschuhe
tennis shoes

Ich kaufe im Einkaufszentrum ein.
I shop at the shopping center (mall).

Anne:	Wohin gehst du?	Where are you going?
Kurt:	Zum Einkaufszentrum.	To the shopping center.
Anne:	Was kaufst du dort?	What are you going to buy there?
Kurt:	Tennisschuhe.	Tennis shoes.

❀❀❀❀❀

Verkäufer:	Guten Morgen! Was darf es sein?	Good morning! May I help you?
Kundin:	Ich möchte ein Buch kaufen.	I would like to buy a book.
Verkäufer:	Gut. Unsere Auswahl ist sehr groß.	Good. Our selection is very large.

 Wer zuerst kommt, mahlt zuerst. First come, first served.

Kunde:	Wie viel kostet diese CD?	How much is this CD?
Kassiererin:	Sie kostet 16 Euro.	It costs 16 euro.
Kunde:	Das ist teuer!	That's expensive!
Kassiererin:	Nein, das ist billig.	No, that's cheap.
Kunde:	Gut. Ich kaufe die CD. Hier ist das Geld.	OK. I'll buy the CD. Here is the money.
Kassiererin:	Danke schön. Da ist Ihr Kleingeld.	Thank you very much. There's your change.

| Verkäuferin: | Noch etwas? | Anything else? |
| Kunde: | Hm...drei Tomaten, fünf Pfirsiche und grüne Bohnen. Ja, das ist alles. | Uhm...three tomatoes, five peaches and green beans. Yes, that's all. |

Exercises

A Match the name of the place in column B with what you can buy there in column A.

	A			B
1.	Tennisschuhe	_____	a.	market
2.	grüne Bohnen	_____	b.	shoe store
3.	CD	_____	c.	furniture store
4.	Stuhl	_____	d.	stationery store
5.	Kulis und Hefte	_____	e.	music store

B Ergänze jeden Satz mit dem Wort für das Bild!

1. Ich möchte _____

   kaufen.

2. Frau Lopez kauft viel Obst auf dem

   _____ .

3. Ich gehe zum

_____ .

4. Hier ist Ihr _____ ,

Herr Hoffmann.

5. Die CD ist billig. Sie kostet 13

_____ .

C Choose the word from the following list that completes each sentence correctly.

Kleingeld   Eis   Geld   kaufen

teuer   geht   kosten

Timo möchte eine CD _____ . Er

_____ zum Einkaufszentrum. Die CDs

_____ heute nur acht Euro. Das ist nicht

_____ . Timo hat zehn Euro. Die Verkäuferin gibt

Timo zwei Euro _____ . Er geht dann in ein Café und

kauft dort für zwei Euro ein _____ . Jetzt hat Timo

kein _____ mehr.

D Wähle die richtige Antwort!

1. If you see the sign "reduzierter Preis," how would you expect the price of the object to be?
   a. billig   c. schön
   b. teuer   d. grün

2. What do you reply if the cashier says "Das macht 55 Euro"?
   a. Wo ist das Geschäft?   c. Hier ist das Geld.
   b. Ich kaufe auf dem Markt ein.   d. Was kaufst du dort?

3. What do you get back if you give the cashier too much money?
   a. Auswahl   c. Markt
   b. Kasse   d. Kleingeld

4. Who helps you find what you need?
   a. der Verkäufer oder die   c. der Kassierer oder die Kassiererin
      Verkäuferin
   b. der Kunde oder die Kundin   d. der Landwirt oder die Landwirtin

5. What do you say if you want to find out about the price?
   a. Wie viel Uhr ist es?   c. Wie viel Geld haben Sie?
   b. Wie viel kostet es?   d. Wie viel ist neun und zwölf?

E Welche Antwort ist richtig?

1. Noch etwas?
   a. Ja. Ich spiele Fußball.
   b. Ja. Ein Buch, bitte.
   c. Nein. Ich habe Geld.
   d. Nein. Ich kaufe im Geschäft ein.

2. Warum gehst du auf den Markt?
   a. Ich möchte Bananen und Birnen kaufen.
   b. Dort gibt es keine Auswahl.
   c. Es ist da sehr teuer.
   d. Ich komme mit.

3. Ist die CD teuer?
   a. Ja. Es ist eine CD.
   b. Nein. Sie ist billig.
   c. Nein. Sie ist schön.
   d. Ja. Sie ist groß.

4. Wie viel kosten die Tennisschuhe?
   a. Eine Auswahl.
   b. Ein reduzierter Preis.
   c. Viele Pfirsiche.
   d. Viel Geld.

5. Was darf es sein?
   a. Ich habe kein Kleingeld.
   b. Nein, das ist nicht billig.
   c. Ich möchte ein Heft kaufen.
   d. Das kostet viel Geld.

F You are in a clothing store. Complete the conversation between you, the customer, and the salesclerk.

Verkäufer: Guten Tag.

Du: Guten _____ .

Verkäufer: Was darf es _____ , bitte?

Du: Ich _____ ein Hemd kaufen.

Verkäufer: Hier _____ unsere Auswahl. Sie ist sehr groß.

Du: Dieses Hemd hier hat eine schöne _____ .

Verkäufer: Ja, blau ist sehr schön.

Du: Wie viel kostet das _____ ?

Verkäufer: Nur 19 _____ . Heute ist es ein

reduzierter _____ .

Du: Gut. Ich _____ es.

Verkäufer: Prima. Die _____ ist dort.

Kreuzworträtsel

G

Vertical

1. "Herr Pigini wohnt in Berlin. ...kommt aus Italien."
2. "Das Haus kostet viel...."
3. "reduzierter..."
4. "Frau Lehmann hat viele Kleider. ...hat eine große Auswahl."
5. a popular place for buying fruits and vegetables
6. "Wie viel...diese CD?"
7. "Die Auswahl im Einkaufszentrum ist sehr...." (ß = SS)
8. "Wo ist...Kasse?"
12. "Ich...im Geschäft ein."
13. "Willi kauft Bananen, Birnen und grüne...."
17. "In diesem Geschäft gibt es eine große...."
18. "...gehst du jetzt? Auf den Markt."
19. "Ist der Computer billig? Nein, er ist...."
20. "...kaufe heute ein."

Horizontal

3. "Obst"
6. one or more coins
9. the opposite of "hier"
10. "...kostet 50 Euro."
11. "Renate hat...schönes Kleid."
12. it contains coins and bills
14. "Herr Kinski ist...Kassierer in diesem Geschäft."
15. "...ist der Markt?"
16. "...Einkaufszentrum ist in der Stadt."
19. what you need to play a certain kind of sport
21. the person waited on by a salesclerk
22. "Maria und Natascha gehen um acht Uhr...die Klasse."
23. the opposite of "dort" or "da"
24. "Ist das Hemd teuer? Nein, es ist...."

DER BOHLENPLATZ

die Einkaufsmeile beim Universitäts-Klinikum

... es gibt viel zu entdecken
in über 150 Läden rund um den Bohlenplatz
und all seinen Seitengassen.

Entdecken Sie die Vielfalt
und den Charme der kleinen Läden.

Elster-Trachten

- Trachten und
Landhausmode -

Johann-Christoph-
Hilf-Str. 24a
(nach Ortskolonnade)
08645 Bad Elster
Telefon: 03 74 37/4 67 29

BEI UNS FINDEN
SIE EINE GROSSE
AUSWAHL VON
MODELLEN
BEKANNTER
FIRMEN, WIE

GEIGER Collections   COUNTRY Line

SPORTALM   Perry   JULIUS LANG®

CITY CENTER FÜRTH

"Für uns
keine Frage: Das

Einkaufserlebnis

ist das City-Center. Dort finden
wir alles, was einen
Einkaufsbummel erst richtig schön
macht."

Leute, Laune, Leben – immer etwas los !

Kids in´s Kinderland.
Parken in der Tiefgarage.

Frauendorfer

POLSTERMÖBEL + KUNSTGEWERBE

91054 ERLANGEN · BOHLENPLATZ 24
GEORG FRAUENDORFER · POLSTERMEISTER

ERLANGENS FÜHRENDES FACHGESCHÄFT FÜR MARIONETTEN UND BÄREN
GESCHENKE UND MITBRINGSEL IN GROSSER AUSWAHL
AUFPOLSTERN UND NEUBEZUG VON POLSTERMÖBELN, ECKBÄNKEN, STÜHLEN, ETC. IN EIGENER WERKSTATT

FON 09131/2 36 57

Wie reist du?

How do you travel?

Ich fliege.
I travel by plane.

Ich fahre mit dem Bus.
I travel by bus.

Ich fahre mit dem Auto.
I travel by car.

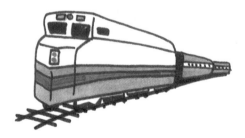

Ich fahre mit dem Zug.
I travel by train.

Ich fahre mit dem Schiff.
I travel by ship.

 Reisen bildet.   Whoever travels far knows much.

die Angestellte
clerk

auf dem Flughafen
at the airport

der Reisepaß
passport

der Koffer
suitcase

der Schalter
ticket counter

der Reisende
traveler

Angestellte:	Ihren Reisepass, bitte?	Your passport, please?
Reisender:	Er ist in meinem Koffer.	It's in my suitcase.
Angestellte:	Sie brauchen ihn, wenn Sie ankommen...bei der Passkontrolle.	You'll need it when you arrive...at passport control.
Reisender:	Gut. Wo steht das Flugzeug?	OK. Where is the plane?
Angestellte:	Am Flugsteig 20. Dort drüben rechts. Gute Reise.	At gate 20. Over there, to the right. Have a nice trip.

Reisende:	Um wie viel Uhr fährt der nächste Zug nach Berlin?	What time does the next train for Berlin leave?
Angestellter:	Um zwölf Uhr. Hier ist der Fahrplan.	At twelve o'clock. Here's the schedule.
Reisende:	Danke. Ich möchte eine Rückfahrkarte, zweite Klasse.	I'd like a round-trip ticket, second class.
Angestellter:	Hier ist Ihre Fahrkarte. Das macht 90 Euro.	Here's your ticket. It's 90 euro.

Herr Bodo:	Entschuldigen Sie. Wie komme ich zum Hotel Krone?	Excuse me. How do I get to Hotel Krone?
Frau Meier:	Fahren Sie mit dem Bus Nummer 2 und steigen Sie am Park aus. Das Hotel ist links.	Take bus number 2 and get off at the park. The hotel is on the left.

Exercises

A Verbinde B mit A.

<table>
<tr><td colspan="2">A</td><td colspan="2">B</td></tr>
<tr><td>1.</td><td>Gute Reise.</td><td>a.</td><td>Excuse me.</td></tr>
<tr><td>2.</td><td>Entschuldigen Sie.</td><td>b.</td><td>Over there, to the right.</td></tr>
<tr><td>3.</td><td>Sie brauchen einen Reisepass.</td><td>c.</td><td>The plane is at the gate.</td></tr>
<tr><td></td><td></td><td>d.</td><td>Here's a schedule.</td></tr>
<tr><td>4.</td><td>Zweite Klasse, bitte.</td><td>e.</td><td>Get off at the park.</td></tr>
<tr><td>5.</td><td>Dort drüben, rechts.</td><td>f.</td><td>You need a passport.</td></tr>
<tr><td>6.</td><td>Steigen Sie am Park aus.</td><td>g.</td><td>Second class, please.</td></tr>
<tr><td>7.</td><td>Ich möchte eine Rückfahrkarte.</td><td>h.</td><td>Have a nice trip.</td></tr>
<tr><td>8.</td><td>Es ist links.</td><td>i.</td><td>I'd like a round-trip ticket.</td></tr>
<tr><td>9.</td><td>Hier ist ein Fahrplan.</td><td>j.</td><td>It's on the left.</td></tr>
<tr><td>10.</td><td>Das Flugzeug steht am Flugsteig.</td><td></td><td></td></tr>
</table>

B Wie reist du? Ergänze die Sätze auf Deutsch!

1. Ich _____ .

2. Ich _____ .

3. Ich _____ .

4. Ich _____ .

5. Ich _____ .

C Wähle die richtige Antwort.

1. Where do you find a train?
   a. auf dem Flughafen
   b. auf dem Bahnhof
   c. bei der Passkontrolle
   d. auf der Straße

2. What do you ask if you want to buy a round-trip ticket?
   a. Ich möchte eine Fahrkarte.
   b. Ich möchte einen Reisepass.
   c. Ich möchte eine Passkontrolle.
   d. Ich möchte eine Rückfahrkarte.

3. What would you look at to find the times when trains, buses, planes, etc. arrive and leave?
   a. der Fahrplan
   b. der Bahnhof
   c. der Flughafen
   d. der Koffer

4. Where do you go at the airport to ask for information and to check your luggage?
   a. das Flugzeug
   b. die Straße
   c. der Schalter
   d. die Passkontrolle

5. If you don't want a first-class ticket, what do you say?
   a. Hier ist der Fahrplan.
   b. Bus Nummer 2.
   c. Dort drüben, rechts.
   d. Zweite Klasse.

D Schreib die Wörter richtig.

1. GIUFLESTG _____

2. FEFKOR _____

3. PFNARAHL _____

4. CTRLSAHE _____

5. HFBAOHN _____

E Lies den Absatz und beantworte dann die Fragen.

Das Wetter ist heute warm und sonnig. Monika und Holger sind am Schalter im Hamburger Bahnhof. Sie sind froh. Sie machen heute eine Reise nach Köln. Holger bleibt bei den Koffern und Monika kauft zwei Fahrkarten. Dann gehen sie zum Bahnsteig, wo der Zug steht. Die Freunde steigen ein. Im Zug sitzt Monika am Fenster. Holger findet einen Platz am Gang. Auf der Reise sprechen sie von ihrem Besuch in Köln. Dort besuchen sie ihre Freunde. Monikas Onkel und Tante wohnen in Bonn, nicht weit von Köln entfernt. In Köln gibt es viel zu sehen und zu tun. Sie fahren fünf Stunden und kommen um vier Uhr im Kölner Bahnhof an. Dann steigen sie aus.

eine Reise machen	to take a trip
bleiben	to stay
der Bahnsteig	platform
der Platz am Gang	seat on the aisle
der Besuch	visit
nicht weit entfernt	not far away

1. Wie ist das Wetter?
   - a. schön
   - b. schlecht
   - c. nicht gut
   - d. kalt

2. Wo sind Monika und Holger?
   - a. auf dem Flughafen
   - b. auf dem Bahnhof
   - c. im Auto
   - d. im Flugzeug

3. Wie viele Fahrkarten kauft Monika?
   - a. eine
   - b. zwei
   - c. drei
   - d. vier

4. Wo steht der Zug?
   - a. am Fenster
   - c. am Schalter
   - c. am Bahnsteig
   - d. am Gang

5. Wo steigen Monika und Holger aus?
   - a. in Hamburg
   - b. in Köln
   - c. in Bonn
   - d. in Zürich

F Complete the analogies.

1. kaufen: Kunde = _____ : Reisender

2. Bahnhof: _____ = Flughafen: Flugzeug

3. Schiff: Ozean = Bus: _____

4. Flugsteig: Flughafen = _____ : Bahnhof

Kreuzworträtsel

Vertical

G

1. Sie brauchen Ihren Reisepass bei der....
2. Um wie viel Uhr fährt der nächste...nach Hamburg?
3. "Zehn" auf Englisch.
4. Sie brauchen den Reisepass, wenn Sie...kommen.
5. ...wie viel Uhr beginnt das Konzert?
7. Die...steht am Schalter.
10. Ich finde einen Platz am....
11. Das Flugzeug steht am...20.
12. "Gehen" auf Englisch.
13. "Nein" auf Englisch.
18. Der Zug steht schon auf dem....
21. Holger und Monika sind.... Sie machen heute eine Reise.
24. "Sohn" auf Englisch.

Horizontal

1. Holger findet einen...am Gang.
6. Die Freunde steigen in den Bus....
7. Der Zug steht...Bahnsteig.
8. ...Sie am Park aus.
9. Der Reisepass ist...meinem Koffer.
11. Dort stehen viele Flugzeuge.
14. "Gut" auf englisch.
15. Heute ist es...heiß.
16. Monika...Holger fahren nach Köln.
17. Wie geht es Ihnen, Herr Böhme? ..., danke.
19. Dieter wohnt in Hamburg. ...ist 16 Jahre alt.
20. Wenn du nach Deutschland fliegst, dann brauchst du einen....
22. Der Teller, die Tasse und das Glas stehen auf dem....
23. ...ist heute warm und sonnig.
25. Wohin fliegt Herr Lehmann? ...fliegt nach München.
26. Die Freunde möchten im Sommer nach^ Österreich....

CISALPINO · SBB CFF FFS

RMV
Es gelten die Gemeinsamen Beförderungsbedingungen und Tarifbestimmungen
Einzelfahrt Erwachsene ermäßigt
Datum 13.10.02 Uhrzeit 10
von Ffm-Nied Hst.-Nr. 56102
nach
Tarifgebiet 50
über direkter Weg Autom. Nr. 03
Preis 1.50 €
incl. 7% MwSt. Preis-St. 3
DB Deutsche Bahn

ZOLL
DOUANE

Liefer-
verkehr
frei

Parkschein
=
Fahrschein

Parken Sie Ihr Auto auf einem der öffentlichen Parkplätze, lösen Sie Ihren Parkschein, **steigen Sie um in den Bus** und lassen Sie sich in die City chauffieren.
Selbstverständlich kostenlos!

Während der gesamten Parkzeit können Sie in der Erlanger Innenstadt alle Busse nutzen, soft Sie möchten – natürlich auch wieder zurück zum Parkplatz.

Den genauen Geltungsbereich des **City-Sondertarifs** entnehmen Sie den Hinweisen an den Haltestellen.

VGN
Verkehrsverbund Großraum Nürnberg

ESTW
ERLANGER STADTWERKE
Partner im VGN